D0608168

The **Princeton Review**®

Reading & Writing Workout for the
SAT®

on

This Book Was Purchased With
Funds Generated By
The Library's Passport Center

sac
l**b** SACRAMENTO PUBLIC LIBRARY

n Review

iew.com

Penguin
Random
House

The Princeton Review
110 E. 42nd Street, 7th Floor
New York, NY 10017
E-mail: editorialsupport@review.com

Copyright © 2019 by TPR Education IP Holdings, LLC.
All rights reserved.

Published in the United States by Penguin Random House LLC, New York, and in Canada by Random House of Canada, a division of Penguin Random House Ltd., Toronto.

Some content excerpted and reprinted with the following permissions:

"Frank Lloyd Wright—Twenty Years After His Death," *The New York Times,* April 15, 1979.

DINNER AT THE HOMESICK RESTAURANT by Anne Tyler, copyright © 1982 by Anne Tyler Modarressi. Used by permission of Alfred A. Knopf, an imprint of the Knopf Doubleday Publishing Group, a division of Penguin Random House LLC. All rights reserved. Any third party use of this material, outside of this publication, is prohibited. Interested parties must apply directly to Penguin Random House LLC for permission.

THE RAREST OF THE RARE: VANISHING ANIMALS, TIMELESS WORLDS by Diane Ackerman, 1995. Used by permission of Random House, an imprint and division of Penguin Random House LLC. All rights reserved. Any third party use of this material, outside of this publication, is prohibited. Interested parties must apply directly to Penguin Random House LLC for permission.

I KNOW WHY THE CAGED BIRD SINGS by Maya Angelou, copyright © 1969 and renewed 1997 by Maya Angelou. Used by permission of Random House, an imprint and division of Penguin Random House LLC. All rights reserved. Any third party use of this material, outside of this publication, is prohibited. Interested parties must apply directly to Penguin Random House LLC for permission."

Who grows your food? (And why it matters), an article by Bob Schildgen that originally appeared in the November/December 2004 issue of Sierra magazine. www.sierramagazine.org.

Terms of Service: The Princeton Review Online Companion Tools ("Student Tools") for retail books are available for only the two most recent editions of that book. Student Tools may be activated only twice per eligible book purchased for two consecutive 12-month periods, for a total of 24 months of access. Activation of Student Tools more than twice per book is in direct violation of these Terms of Service and may result in discontinuation of access to Student Tools Services.

ISBN: 978-0-525-56794-3
eBook ISBN: 978-0-525-56798-1
ISSN: 1551-6423

Editorial
Rob Franek, Editor-in-Chief
Craig Patches, Director of Production
Deborah Weber, Production Design Manager
Selena Coppock, Managing Editor
Meave Shelton, Senior Editor
Sarah Litt, Editor
Orion McBean, Editor
Aaron Riccio, Editor

Random House Publishing Team
Tom Russell, VP, Publisher
Alison Stoltzfus, Publishing Director
Ellen Reed, Production Manager
Amanda Yee, Associate Managing Editor
Suzanne Lee, Designer

SAT is a trademark registered by the College Board, which is not affiliated with, and does not endorse, this product.

The Princeton Review is not affiliated with Princeton University.

Editor: Sarah Litt
Production Editors: Jim Melloan and Kathy G. Carter
Production Artist: Deborah Weber

Printed in the United States of America.

10 9 8 7 6 5 4 3 2 1

Fourth Edition

Acknowledgments

This book could not have been built without the hard work of Amy Minster, Elizabeth Owens, Alice Swan, Chris Aylward, Grace Cannon, Gina Donegan, Susan Swinford, Krissi Taylor Leslie, Lori DesRochers, Cat Healey, Sara Soriano, Stefan Maisnier, Bobby Hood, Joelle Cotham, Anthony Krupp, and Jonathan Chiu.

Additionally, The Princeton Review would like to thank Deborah Weber for her laudatory layouts throughout this book, and Jim Melloan and Kathy Carter for their diligent, detailed work with its contents.

Special thanks to Adam Robinson, who conceived of and perfected the Joe Bloggs approach to standardized tests and many of the other successful techniques used by the Princeton Review.

Contents

Get More (Free) Content

1 Go to **PrincetonReview.com/cracking.**

2 Enter the following ISBN for your book: 9780525567943.

3 Answer a few simple questions to set up an exclusive Princeton Review account. (If you already have one, you can just log in.)

4 Click the "Student Tools" button, also found under "My Account" from the top toolbar. You're all set to access your bonus content!

Need to report a potential **content** issue?

Contact **EditorialSupport@review.com.**
Include:

- full title of the book
- ISBN
- page number

Need to report a **technical** issue?

Contact **TPRStudentTech@review.com**
and provide:

- your full name
- email address used to register the book
- full book title and ISBN
- computer OS (Mac/PC) and browser (Firefox, Safari, etc.)

The Princeton Review®

Once you've registered, you can...

- Find any late-breaking information released about the SAT

- Get valuable advice about the college application process, including tips for writing a great essay and where to apply for financial aid

- If you're still choosing between colleges, use our searchable rankings of *The Best 384 Colleges* to find out more information about your dream school

- Check to see if there have been any corrections or updates to this edition

Look For These Icons Throughout The Book

PROVEN TECHNIQUES

APPLIED STRATEGIES

MORE GREAT BOOKS

Chapter 1
Introduction

READ THIS STUFF FIRST

Wouldn't it be great if all the problems on the Writing and Language section of the SAT looked like this?

While the SAT may seem like a tricky test, the answers are right in front of **1** you. Finding the right answer doesn't mean you need to know all the grammar rules or **2** have read all the books ever written. You just need to know where to **3** put your eyes for the correct answer!

1

A) NO CHANGE

B) Just bubble A.

C) You're welcome.

D) <3, College Board

2

A) NO CHANGE

B) to have read

C) to read

D) This one's hard. Freebie! Just pick anything!

3

A) NO CHANGE

B) put your eyes on

C) look with your eyes

D) look (trust us, it's this one)

Only in our dreams is the College Board, which creates and manages the administration of the SAT, ever this nice. But believe it or not, the test writers do provide clues to every question you'll encounter on the SAT. This workbook is here to show you how to find those clues and the traps the writers set for test takers so that you can get every point you deserve in the Reading and Writing and Language portions of the test—and maybe even a few extra points.

For Reading, we'll show you how to quickly and accurately find correct answers without getting too bogged down. You'll learn how to efficiently find answers in the passage without actually reading the whole passage and how to avoid traps in the answer choices. For Writing and Language, we'll teach you the strategies and grammar rules you will need to handle any question you face. And for the Essay, we'll tell you all the most important things that graders are looking for in top-scoring essays. Throughout, you'll find test-like passages written in the style of the SAT to give you ample opportunities to practice the comprehension skills needed for the test.

Though the SAT went through a bit of a makeover recently, the techniques and strategies you'll learn throughout this book have passed the test of time. They are not based solely on our opinions and theories; they've been proven by the students who have taken our SAT courses over the past 30 years and have been adapted to make sure you're ready for this latest version of the SAT.

So let's get started!

VERBAL SKILLS = 50% OF THE SAT

The SAT has four scored sections (not including the optional Essay); the first half tests your Verbal skills. This book will help you with what's tested in the Reading and Writing and Language sections of the test. If you're looking for help with the Math, as well, never fear! Check out *Math Workout for the SAT*.

Here's what the Verbal section looks like:

- One 65-minute Reading section
  - 52 passage-based questions
  - 5 passages
    - 10–11 questions per passage; order of passages may vary
    - One U.S./World Literature passage
    - Two History/Social Studies passages
    - Two Science passages
- One 35-minute Writing and Language section
  - 44 passage-based questions
  - 4 passages

HOW THE SAT IS SCORED

For each question you answer correctly on the SAT, you'll receive one raw point, period. There's no penalty for leaving questions blank or answering them incorrectly, so you can only improve your raw score by guessing.

Your Evidence-Based Reading & Writing (EBRW) section score combines your raw scores from both areas, so out of the 52 Reading questions and 44 Writing and Language questions, you can gain up to 96 raw points. This total raw score is then converted to a scaled score falling between 200 and 800 points. These scores are reported in 10-point increments, so you could score a 510 or a 520, but not a 515. This, in turn, makes up half of your total score. To get that total, simply add your EBRW score to your Math score.

What We Say About the Essay
Your Essay is optional and scored separately, so you don't have to worry about it having an impact on your total.

When you receive your scores, you'll notice a number of other scores as well. These are your "test" scores, "cross-test" scores, and "subscores." For Verbal, your test scores refer to the Reading and Writing and Language sections individually and are reported on a scale of 10–40. The two cross-test scores are also reported on a scale of 10–40 but cover questions that fall into the category of "Analysis in Science" or "Analysis of History/Social Studies." These questions can appear in any of the tests, including the Math test. Lastly, the subscores tallied within the Reading and Writing and Language sections are Expression of Ideas, Standard English Conventions, Words in Context, and Command of Evidence. Each of these is reported on a scale of 1–15.

WHAT'S A GOOD SCORE

Simply put, a good score is the one that gets you into the college of your dreams.

So, what's your first step to figuring out what's a good score for *you*? Start doing some research! Make a list of the schools you'd most like to attend and look into their average/median scores to get an idea of what you'll need to score to be considered for admission (we're a bit biased, but we've heard www.princetonreview.com and *The Best 384 Colleges* are both great resources for college research). From there, take a practice test and start putting a plan in place to hit your goal score. While colleges consider a LOT of factors when making admissions decisions, your SAT results are a big factor, and can be just what you need to get your foot in the door at the school of your dreams. The following table doesn't have exact numbers, as the College Board makes individual adaptations each year, but you can use it as a best approximation of how your raw scores from this book might look on the actual SAT.

RAW SCORE CONVERSION TABLE SECTION AND TEST SCORES

Raw Score (# of correct answers)	Math Section Score	Reading Test Score	Writing and Language Test Score	Raw Score (# of correct answers)	Math Section Score	Reading Test Score	Writing and Language Test Score
0	200	10	10	30	530	27	29
1	200	10	10	31	530	27	30
2	210	10	10	32	540	28	31
3	230	10	10	33	550	28	31
4	250	11	11	34	550	29	32
5	260	12	12	35	560	29	32
6	280	13	12	36	570	30	33
7	290	14	13	37	580	30	34
8	310	15	14	38	590	31	34
9	320	15	15	39	590	31	35
10	330	16	15	40	600	32	36
11	350	17	16	41	610	32	36
12	360	17	17	42	620	33	37
13	370	18	18	43	630	34	39
14	380	18	18	44	640	35	40
15	390	19	19	45	650	35	
16	400	20	19	46	660	36	
17	420	20	20	47	670	37	
18	430	21	21	48	680	37	
19	430	21	22	49	680	38	
20	440	22	22	50	690	39	
21	450	22	23	51	700	39	
22	460	23	24	52	720	40	
23	470	23	25	53	730		
24	480	24	25	54	740		
25	490	24	26	55	760		
26	500	25	26	56	770		
27	510	25	27	57	790		
28	510	26	28	58	800		
29	520	26	29				

CONVERSION EQUATION SECTION AND TEST SCORES

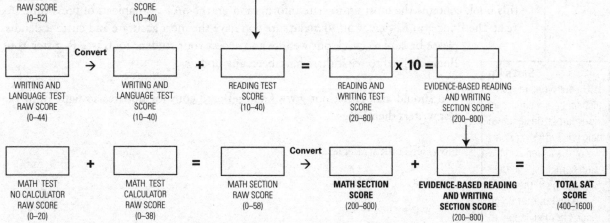

CAN I REALLY IMPROVE ON THE SAT?

In short, YES! You just have to slightly shift the way you look at the test. It's all about getting more questions right, right? That means not getting frustrated on the Verbal section by trying to figure out the "best" answers and managing with the limited time constraints. Instead, we'll show you how to efficiently spot what the College Board is looking for in a correct answer, recognize how they make bad answers look so enticing, and know what's worth spending time on, thereby increasing your total number of raw points.

WHAT IS THE PRINCETON REVIEW?

The Princeton Review is one of the nation's premier test-preparation companies. We give courses in more than 500 locations and online, and publish best-selling books and software to prepare students for this test. Over the last 35 years, we have also helped to prepare students for the PSAT/NMSQT, ACT, GRE, GMAT, LSAT, MCAT, and other standardized tests.

The Princeton Review's techniques are unique and powerful. We developed them after spending countless hours scrutinizing real SATs, analyzing them with computers, and proving our theories with real students.

This book is based on our extensive experience in the classroom. Our techniques for cracking the SAT will help you improve your SAT scores by teaching you to:

1. think like the test writers at the College Board
2. take full advantage of the time allowed
3. find the answers to questions you don't understand by guessing intelligently
4. avoid the traps that the College Board has laid for you (and use those traps to your advantage)

A NOTE TO OUR STUDENTS

This book contains the most up-to-date information on the SAT available as of press time. As we at The Princeton Review want to make sure you have the most accurate and current details, please be sure to check our website and access your student tools (see Register Your Book Online) to see if there have been any updates.

You should also check out www.CollegeBoard.com for updates straight from the test writers themselves.

Now, let's talk strategies.

Surf's Up
On our website, you'll also find a bunch of cool resources designed to help you with every part of the college admissions process. The best SAT scores in the world won't matter if you don't actually apply to any schools!

Chapter 2
Strategies

THE ART OF ELIMINATION
Take a look at the following example.

I

> What does the word "strategy" mean in the context of the passage?

Kind of tough to answer this question without the context of the passage, isn't it? While the College Board, the company behind the SAT, isn't known for fairness, rest assured that you'll never be asked a question like that. But what if I told you that you could still get the question right without the passage? "How?" you might ask. Well, let's take a look at the question again, this time with something the College Board always provides on the Verbal portion of the SAT, the answers.

I

> What does the word "strategy" mean in the context of the passage?
>
> A) peacocks
> B) working smart to improve your SAT score
> C) the Philippines
> D) five

It's much easier once you have the answer choices to consider! You're still unlikely to see a question like this one on the SAT, but checking the choices is always the first and most important strategy to use if you want to improve your score. It's all about the Process of Elimination (POE). The correct answer is right there in front of you; you just need to get rid of the bad answers. For each and every question on the Verbal portion of the SAT, there are three incorrect answers, which means that 75% of the test is garbage. Your task: start taking out the trash!

Bad answers are all over the test and they're generally easier to spot than the correct (and often very well hidden) answer. By starting with the answer choices and eliminating the ones that you know are wrong, you increase your chance of getting the question correct. Whenever you see an answer that can't be correct, cross it out with a slash. If it looks right, put a check next to it and keep reading. If it looks like it might be true, but you aren't sure, put a ~ mark next to it. We will refer to these three marks (slash, check, and ~) as POE symbols.

GUESSING IS GOOD (I.E., LEAVE NO BLANKS)

Using the process of elimination on this test means that, even if you're not 100% sure your answer is the correct one, you're able to make an educated guess and earn a raw point you might not have otherwise earned. But what about those questions that you either aren't able to eliminate any answers on or that are too time-consuming? Since there's no penalty for getting a question wrong on the SAT, regardless of whether you're able to eliminate any answers or not, always have your **LOTD (Letter of the Day)** at the ready for questions you don't know how to do, don't want to do, or simply don't have time to do.

Here's how LOTD works. **Pick one letter and stick to it throughout the test!** Since there are just as many As as there are Bs, Cs, and Ds, by maintaining a consistent guessing letter, you have a much better chance of picking up a few free raw points than if you were to guess at random. And, let's be honest: if you find yourself running out of time, scoring a few extra points without even reading a question is pretty awesome.

PACING

When you're under the pressure of a timed test, every point counts, but stressing about getting to every single question could actually be the worst thing you can do. When the clock is involved, you may unintentionally find the quickest way to do the "wrongest" thing, the proverbial "careless mistake." And what's worse than coming to an easy question, a question you KNOW you should get right, working through it too quickly, and getting it wrong because you misread it? Is it better to attempt all 5 of the passages if you get only 50% of the questions right, or would it be better to do just 4 passages and focus on accuracy to get 75% of those questions correct? Right there, you'd already be scoring 4 or 5 more points doing less work with option #2. And don't forget about your LOTD! Guessing on that last passage will pick up another extra point or two, meaning that working smarter, rather than harder, actually pays off big!

So pacing is not about figuring out how to get to every question; it's about doing the right number of questions for YOU! Mastering the art of effective pacing takes practice, but it's all about finding the number of questions you need to answer correctly in order to hit your goal score.

PERSONAL ORDER OF DIFFICULTY

Working hand-in-hand with your pacing is your Personal Order of Difficulty, or POOD. The SAT's Verbal section isn't arranged in order of difficulty, which means that you should take a moment to skim the contents and choose passages that you feel most comfortable with. The same goes for each set of questions. Certain types of questions may come more naturally to you than others, and because they're all worth the same number of points, you might as well get the ones you can more easily attack out of the way before potentially getting stuck on tougher questions.

Remember, this is all about hitting your pacing goal, so let your POOD speak to you. If history or literature bores you, you might want to skip to the science passages first. If you come to a weird question about the order of sentences that might take a while, make a note to come back and skip it for now. (Don't forget to fill in your LOTD if you run out of time!)

Take control of the test as much as you can. You don't have a choice about the order of the tests themselves—it's always Reading, then Writing and Language, followed by Math, and the Essay (if you choose to take it). But within each individual test, the ordering is all up to you. There are 52 questions in the Reading Test. If question 10 trips you up and you're unable to make any sense of what the passage is even saying, are you going to stick with that question and not attempt the rest of the section? No way! Look to play up your strengths and minimize your weaknesses. Spend time where you're most likely to score points!

So many individual factors go into building and understanding your POOD; that's why it's your *Personal* Order of Difficulty. As you're practicing, make sure you're keeping an eye out for the questions that take a long time or are just plain confusing, and save those for later. Do the questions that you're able to answer efficiently and accurately: those made easier using our techniques.

You may be able to answer some questions in just a few seconds, while others may seem to last a lifetime. Prepare yourself to be able to identify those instances and know when to stick with the question and when it's time to move on to the next one.

YOUR PENCIL

There's no question about it: the Reading Test is long and the Writing and Language Test is rushed. With so much going on in so little time, you need every tool at your disposal to take down this test. That's why it's imperative that your pencil ALWAYS be moving. Whether it's crossing out bad answers, underlining key information in the passage, or bubbling in answers a passage at a time, it all comes down to keeping you actively engaged in what you are doing. One of the easiest ways to start increasing your SAT score is to jot things down in the test book, by the questions, in the margins, next to the answer choices, and so on. Don't try to keep everything in your head: that's what the test makers want you to do. Using that pencil to leave reminders or to call out relevant details is a key step for reaching your pacing goals. Every note helps to keep you focused and one step ahead of the test.

Everything about this test, from the length to the passage selections and the questions and answers, is designed to put you through the wringer. Take control of the test and use everything available to you to make this test a little easier. Remember the Ps and embrace your POE, pacing, POOD, and pencil.

A CHANGE WILL DO YOU GOOD

The practice in this workbook is designed to help you find the best way for you to take the test. But that means you need to be willing to give new methods a chance, especially if you want your score to change. As the saying goes, doing the same thing over and over again with the expectation of different results is the definition of insanity.

Throughout this book, we will introduce you to all of the question types you'll encounter on the SAT and we'll show you how to strategically and systematically approach them to increase your score. Really give these strategies a try; if you don't get it the first time, don't just give up and go back to old habits. You've likely been taking tests for a long time, and it may be hard to approach some of these questions in a different way, but we won't steer you in the wrong direction. Think about learning a new skill to add to something you're already good at: for instance, if you're a golfer learning a new swing or a tennis player learning a new serve. It's not that your old swing or serve didn't serve you well; it got you where you are. But in order to get better, you sometimes need to try things that might seem a little odd. At first, you might not be used to shifting the weight in your hips or adjusting the angle at which your racquet hits the ball, but with practice your new swing or new serve can take you to the next level. It just takes practice.

EVEN THE COLLEGE BOARD KNOWS OUR TECHNIQUES WORK

The College Board and former authors the Educational Testing Service have spent a great deal of time and money over the years trying to persuade people that the SAT can't be cracked. At the same time, the companies have struggled to find ways of changing the SAT so that The Princeton Review won't be able to crack it—in effect acknowledging what our students have known all along, which is that our techniques really do work. Despite the College Board's efforts, the SAT remains highly vulnerable to our techniques. It just takes practice to gain comfort with the approaches.

TAKING CHARGE

When you take the SAT, you have to give up a lot of control. The administrators of the test tell you when to show up. They tell you where to sit. They tell you when to begin and when to stop. They even tell you the specific type of pencil (the number) that you must bring with you.

This is all the more reason, then, to make sure that you take as much control back as possible. You can take charge by preparing ahead of time, using the strategies and techniques we're going to show you in the chapters ahead, learning what is actually going to be on the test, being aggressive, and eliminating wrong answers.

Above all else, keep your sense of perspective. Remember, the SAT is a high-stakes test, but it's totally a BEATABLE test.

Chapter 3
Reading

EVIDENCE-BASED READING

The Reading section is *long*—you have 65 minutes to tackle 5 passages and 52 questions, and the passages aren't exactly drawn from what most would consider a relaxing beach read. That might sound like a recipe for a lot of frantic reading, but it doesn't have to be. Consider the questions below.

5

In line 14, "blotted out" most nearly means

A) blemished

B) obscured

C) extinguished

D) removed

6

The author mentions Sweden and Brazil in order to emphasize which point about the Krakatoa eruption?

A) Although the eruption was devastating in Krakatoa, there were no effects felt in other parts of the word.

B) The volcanic eruption was so powerful that it affected the climate of countries thousands of miles away.

C) Local destruction in Krakatoa was enormous, but the destruction in Europe and South America was, if anything, greater.

D) The explosion would have been even more destructive had it happened today.

Did you notice something super helpful about question 5? Sure enough, the question actually tells you where to look to find the answer! That means that instead of having to read the entire passage in the hopes of finding the answer, you can focus on a much more manageable portion, something that looks more like this:

Line   The eruption of Krakatoa sent clouds of ash and
        dust into Earth's atmosphere to a height of 50 miles.
        The Sun was blotted out entirely for two days within a
15   100-mile radius of the volcano, and Earth temperatures
        as far away as Sweden and Brazil were several degrees
        lower than average that year.

Of course, you also might have noticed that question 6 *doesn't* contain a handy line reference. But while there isn't a line reference, question 6 does still provide a way to narrow down your search in the passage: it asks about *Sweden* and *Brazil*, two words that will likely stand out while skimming the passage. In fact, the portion of the passage you read for question 5 also mentions Sweden and Brazil. Even without a line reference, you could attack question 6 by using key words from the question. In addition, the questions in each passage are asked in roughly chronological order. Therefore, you should look for references to Sweden and Brazil in the portion of the passage after line 14.

In other words, the answers to questions 5 and 6 are located in specific places in the passage, and you don't have to read the entire passage to find the evidence you need to get them right. While the phrase "evidence-based" might *sound* like a lot of extra work, what it actually means is that the answers are in the passage and you can use the questions themselves to help you work efficiently to find the evidence and choose the correct answer.

Your Goal Is to Answer Questions

No matter how much you read, the proctor will not be walking around the examination room, saying, "Ah, Jessica! Excellent reading form. I'm giving you 20 extra points on your Evidence-based Reading score." The only way you get points in SAT Evidence-based Reading is by correctly answering questions.

The sooner you get to the questions, the sooner you start earning points. For example, both of the questions on the previous page could be answered without reading the rest of the passage (which we didn't show you). In question 5, you needed to supply a word that would fit in place of the quoted words "blotted out." The correct answer was (B), "obscured," because the volcanic ash filled the sky to the point that the sun's rays couldn't get through. Even if you had read the entire passage several times and made extensive notes, the answer to this question was based on only one thing: your understanding of this sentence in this paragraph.

The correct answer to question 6, which asked why the author brought up Sweden and Brazil, was (B). In the context of this paragraph, the two countries were mentioned to show just how powerful the eruption had been. Again, even if you had memorized the entire passage, the only place to find the answer to this question was right here in this paragraph.

These questions are pretty typical of the SAT in that they include either a line reference or an identification of the paragraph in which the answer can be found. Most of the Reading questions tell you where to look for the answer because they are arranged in chronological order. The answer to question 16 can be found somewhere between the answers to questions 15 and 17.

They're Too Long!

Many students look at a passage of 500 to 750 words and feel defeated at the thought of trying to keep track of a passage that long—but the situation is much better than they think. Reading passages are actually just a series of paragraphs like the one you just read. You don't need to remember details from the entire passage at once; you just need to focus on the details of one section at a time as you answer the questions dealing with that information. Then you can move on to another section.

The Exception That Proves the Rule
Dual passages, which we'll talk about in a moment, do have some questions that refer to content from both passages. But they also have questions that pertain to each individual passage, and so they can still be tackled, for the most part, in bite-sized chunks.

THE PASSAGES

Subject Areas

Because everybody's Personal Order of Difficulty is different, it's important that you know what types of passages to expect on the test. This will allow you to use your time as efficiently as possible. The five passages will come from three subject areas and will consist of:

- One **US/World Literature** passage drawn from a classic or more recent work of literature
- Two **History/Social Studies** passages drawn from fields such as history, economics, sociology, and political science and from primary historical documents
- Two **Science** passages drawn from work in fields such as earth science, chemistry, and physics and addressing concepts, information, and/or experiments

Other Features

A couple of the passages will also have additional features that could make them *appear* more intimidating.

Dual Passages

One of the History/Social Studies or Science Passages will actually consist of two shorter passages on the same topic. Recent examples of these dual passages have given two views on the subject of mining in space, on the effect of new media on brain development, and on the rights of 18th-century women. Whatever the subject matter of the dual passages you encounter, you should tackle them in the following order:

1. Answer the questions that refer only to the first passage.
2. Answer the questions that refer only to the second passage.
3. Answer the questions that refer to both passages.

Charts, Tables, and Graphs

Two passages in the Reading section will contain one or two of what the College Board calls *informational graphics,* which are charts, tables, and graphs. That means that two of the four history/social studies and science passages will be accompanied by one or two figures that will provide additional information related to the passages. These passages will include a few questions that ask about the data presented in the graphics, either alone or in relation to the information in the passage. These figures might seem like they'll require more work, but the charts, tables, and graphs provided in the Reading section and the questions about them are relatively straightforward.

The bottom line is that neither dual passages nor charts, tables, and graphs should be cause for alarm, and passages that feature them will not necessarily be more difficult than passages that don't.

THE PRINCETON REVIEW METHOD

Once you've chosen and started working on a passage, you want to find the correct answers to the questions as efficiently as possible. Here's how to do that.

Step One, Read the Blurb: The blurb is the introductory sentence or two given before the body of the passage begins. The blurb provides a frame of reference for the content of the passage.

Step Two, Select and Understand a Question: Remember that questions are presented with general ones first, followed by more specific ones in chronological order. Choose a question whose answer is likely easy to locate—for instance, a question that provides a line reference—and then make sure you understand what the question is asking. In fact, most "questions" on the SAT are not questions at all, but open-ended statements. Rewording the statement as an actual question will help you to better understand how to answer it.

Step Three, Read Just What You Need: Many questions will provide line numbers or a lead word that tells you where to look for your answer. If you read about five lines above and five lines below the referenced line or lead word, you should have enough information to answer the question. Read to find the particular phrase, sentence, or set of lines that provide the evidence on which the answer will be based. If you work through the specific questions this way, you should find that by the time you tackle the more general questions, you've gained a fairly good understanding of the passage, even if you didn't read it from start to finish.

Step Four, Predict the Correct Answer: Since the test writers do their best to provide answer choices that look correct, the best way to avoid talking yourself into an appealing but wrong answer is to know exactly what you're looking for before you consider the answer choices. Take the time to answer the question for yourself in terms of the evidence you've found *before* you consider the answer choices. Marking the support for your answer in the passage is a great way to keep track of the information as you move to the next step in the process. It's also important when you're working with paired questions, which will be discussed in more detail later in the chapter.

Step Five, Use Process of Elimination: With each wrong answer you cross off, it gets easier to compare the remaining answers and decide which one correctly answers the question. Eliminate answer choices that don't match your prediction and compare the remaining choices to see which is correct.

Notice that what you're *NOT* doing is tackling the passage first, lessening the possibility that your mind will wander or decide to savor the nuances of the passage irrelevant to the task of the SAT questions. Use the questions to guide you, reading sections of the passage as you need the information in them. Remember that the only way to get points on the test is by correctly answering questions. It's not how much you read, then, but how much you answer.

THE QUESTION TYPES

Line Reference and Lead Word Questions

The Reading questions will be line reference or lead word questions. In each case, the question will tell you where in the passage to look for the answer.

Line reference questions ask you about a part of the passage and tell you to which lines the question refers. These questions will look like one of the following:

> In paragraph 4, why does the author mention Harry McCallan?
>
> The author cites "many interesting creatures" in lines 34–36 in order to . . .

Sometimes, instead of a line or paragraph number, you will be asked about a proper name or important word that will be pretty easy to find in the passage by running your finger down the passage until you come across it.

In either case, you should look back to the passage to find the lines indicated by the question or the lines in which the lead word can be found. It's important to read a little above and a little below the line number mentioned or the line on which the lead word is, to make sure you understand the line in context. Once you've found the relevant evidence in the passage, predict the answer to the question, and then eliminate any answer choices that do not match your prediction.

From time to time, you will see a question that seems specific, even though it has neither a line reference nor a colorful word to help you find the reference in the passage. It's not a bad idea to skip a question like this until after you've answered the rest of the questions and have a better understanding of the passage. Remember, however, that the questions are arranged chronologically. If you're considering question 6, then the information you need to answer it will probably closely follow the information needed to answer question 5 and come before the information needed to answer question 7.

Vocabulary-In-Context Questions

Vocabulary-in-context questions always include line numbers and ask you to identify the best alternative phrasing for a quoted word or phrase. Here's what one of these questions looks like:

> In line 44, "objective" most nearly means...

The thing to bear in mind for these questions is that the College Board often picks words that have more than one meaning, and the words are generally not being used in their primary sense. For example, the College Board's answer to the question above about the meaning of the word "objective" was the word "material"—certainly not the first meaning anyone would think of picking.

If you find yourself running out of time as you get to a Reading passage, then these are the questions to answer first. Not only do they take the least amount of time, but they also require the smallest amount of overall knowledge of the passage.

General Questions

As you've seen, questions that ask about a specific section of the text are easier to answer without reading the entirety of the passage. The targeted reading you'll do to answer those questions will make you more familiar with the passage overall. This means that once you've answered the more specific questions, you'll be in a good position to tackle the more general questions that you skipped over at first.

The general questions will be easy to recognize because they will ask questions like this:

> The main idea of this passage is to
>
> The primary purpose of the passage is to
>
> The passage is best described as
>
> The passage serves primarily to
>
> The author uses the example of the [Krakatoa eruption] primarily to

Save this type of question for last and you'll save yourself a lot of time.

PAIRED QUESTIONS

The Reading section of the SAT has one more wrinkle to the variety of questions you'll see—paired questions. How can you tell if questions are paired? Take a look at this example.

9

Which choice provides the best evidence for the answer to the previous question?

A) Lines 25–27 ("then . . . reading")

B) Lines 31–32 ("It . . . *ate*")

C) Lines 38–40 ("Because . . . actions")

D) Lines 40–44 ("When . . . Nervous")

If somehow there were an error in your test booklet and you couldn't read question 8, would you be able to do anything more than guess on question 9? No, because without question 8, you'd have no idea what kind of evidence you were looking for! Now consider what happens when you can look at question 8 first.

8

The author introduces the "Homeric idea of *ate*" primarily in order to

A) emphasize the difficulty of the books she was reading.

B) suggest that her father had reacted in the same way that Achilles had.

C) provide another way to understand the use of a particular local term.

D) show the relationship between reading Greek literature and feeling anger.

When you have question 8, it's a lot easier to figure out what to do with question 9, which is why we call questions like these *paired questions*. Paired questions are sets of questions in which one question is followed by a second question that asks you to choose which set of lines best supports the answer you chose for the first question.

In this case, questions 8 and 9 are *specific* paired questions, because question 8 asks a specific question and provides strong lead words. To answer this pair of questions, you'd tackle question 8 first, looking in the passage for the phrase "Homeric idea of *ate*" and then searching the lines above and below the phrase to find out why the author introduces that idea. Once you've found and marked the evidence to answer question 8, it's a piece of cake to answer its partner: all you have to do is check which answer choice for question 9 refers to the lines that you used to answer question 8. It's like a two-for-one deal—answer question 8 and you've done the work for question 9 as well!

You will also come across *general* paired questions. In these, answering the first question in the pair requires a sense of the entire passage. Consider the following pair.

33

Of the series of realizations the author describes, the one most significant to his overall understanding of the events is his realization that

A) he has a serious illness.

B) his previous understanding of his genetic history was erroneous.

C) his treatment will be longer and more painful than he'd originally thought.

D) doctors sometimes try to heal a patient's body without taking into account the patient's emotional and intellectual needs.

34

Which choice provides the best evidence for the answer to the previous question?

A) Lines 1–3 ("Modern . . . body")

B) Lines 18–21 ("Thus . . . precocious")

C) Lines 30–32 ("My . . . idea")

D) Lines 47–51 ("Yet . . . phenomenon")

Question 33 is a general question that asks you to identify the most significant of a number of realizations that are discussed throughout the passage. Characteristically, this general question lacks both a line reference and strong key words to help narrow down a search, and the answer choices in question 34 are not concentrated in one part of the passage but are spread throughout the passage.

Though it might seem counterintuitive, the easiest way to tackle general paired questions is to work backward from the second question in the pair, checking the answer choices to see which sets of lines can be connected to any of the answer choices in the first question. If, in this particular instance, lines 1–3 don't refer to any of the realizations identified in the answer choices for question 33, then (A) can be eliminated for question 34. Likewise, if none of the answer choices in 34 support the idea that the author's realization that he has a serious illness is most significant, then (A) can be eliminated from question 33.

To tackle general paired questions, be methodical.

Step One: **Look for connections between the answers**

Check each answer choice in the second question to see if it offers support for an answer choice in the first question. Record any connections you see.

Step Two: **Eliminate any unconnected answers**

Once you have checked all four answers from the second question, cross off any answers in the second question that you can't connect to an answer in the first question. Then cross off any answer in the first question that is not supported by an answer to the second question.

Step Three: **Compare the remaining answers in the first question and POE**

It might take a little practice to make this approach feel more natural, but the practice will definitely pay off!

PACING STRATEGIES FOR READING

The Reading section is a long section with five different passages and 52 questions to get through, but the only thing that counts toward your score is the number of questions you answer correctly. Thus, it pays to be efficient.

- Don't be afraid to skip over a more challenging passage—even if you've started working on it. Do the passages you find easier first.
- Always look to eliminate wrong answers. Even if you can eliminate only one or two answers, you've still increased your odds of getting the question right.
- Don't stay stuck on a hard question—guess and move on. Once you've made your way through the whole section, you can use any remaining time to return to any questions you found tricky.
- Make sure to bubble in an answer for every question. There's no penalty for guessing, so use the LOTD if you need to.

READING CHECKLIST

1. Read the blurb at the beginning of the passage.
2. Answer specific questions first. These include line-reference, lead-word, and vocabulary-in-context questions, as well as specific paired questions. Use chronology when necessary to help narrow down where to search in the passage for an answer.
3. Answer the general questions next, including general paired questions.
4. With dual passages, answer questions relating to the first passage first. Then answer questions relating to the second passage. Save questions that ask about both passages for last.

Keep these techniques in mind as you try the practice passages that follow. First up is a drill using introductory paragraphs to practice techniques. Then you'll have the opportunity to work some passages using the Process of Elimination. Finally, you have four full-length passages so that you can practice thinking about the order in which you tackle the questions, and start identifying the question and passage types that you feel you need more practice with. The answers are given at the end of the exercise.

Short Passage Drills

Questions 1–2 are based on the following passage.

Ben Jonson, a well-known playwright and seventeenth-century contemporary of John Donne, wrote that while "the first poet in the
Line world in some things," Donne nevertheless "for
5 not keeping of an accent, deserved hanging." Donne's generation admired the depth of his feeling, but was puzzled by his often irregular rhythm and obscure references. It was not until the twentieth century and modern movements
10 that celebrated emotion and allusion that Donne really began to be appreciated. Writers such as T. S. Eliot and W. B. Yeats admired the psychological intricacies of a poet who could one moment flaunt his earthly dalliances with his
15 mistress and the next, wretched, implore God to "bend your force, to break, blow, burn, and make me new."

1

The main idea of the paragraph is that

A) poetry is judged by different standards at different times.

B) Jonson misjudged Donne's worth.

C) Donne's poetry was not fully appreciated until hundreds of years after his death.

D) Donne's rough meter prevented him from being understood in his own lifetime.

2

It can be inferred from the passage that W. B. Yeats was

A) uninterested in meter and rhythm.

B) a modern writer.

C) close to T. S. Eliot.

D) interested in imitating Donne's technique.

Questions 3–4 are based on the following passage.

The term "genetic modification" refers to technology that is used to alter the genes of living organisms. Genetically modified organisms
Line are called "transgenic" if genes from different
5 organisms are combined. The most common transgenic organisms are crops of common fruits and vegetables, which are now grown in more than fifty countries. These crops are typically developed for resistance to herbicides, pesticides,
10 and disease, as well as to increase nutritional value. Some of these transgenic crops currently under development might even yield human vaccines. Along with improving nutrition and alleviating hunger, genetic modification of crops
15 may also help to conserve natural resources and improve waste management.

3

The primary purpose of the paragraph is to

A) establish that transgenic crops are safe.

B) critique the process of genetic modification.

C) overcome opposition to genetically modified foods.

D) provide information about transgenic crops.

4

In line 12, the word "yield" most nearly means

A) produce.

B) surrender.

C) give way.

D) replace.

Questions 5–6 are based on the following passage.

In 1782, philosopher J. Hector St. John de Crèvecoeur became the first to apply the word "melting" to a population of immigrants: "Here *Line* individuals of all nations are melted into a new
5 race of men." Crèvecoeur idealized a nation built from individuals who had transcended their origins and embraced a common American ethos: "From involuntary idleness, servile dependence, penury, and useless labour, he has passed to toils
10 of a very different nature, rewarded by ample subsistence. This is an American." While debate raged as to what exactly "melting" meant— diverse peoples coexisting peacefully while maintaining their differences or refashioning
15 themselves to blend indistinguishably into a new, common substance—Crèvecoeur's term was here to stay: America, settled by immigrants, was to have a unified populace.

5

According to the paragraph, "debate raged" (lines 11–12) over whether immigrant groups

A) had the ability to put aside their differences and coexist peacefully.

B) understood what Crèvecoeur originally meant by the term "melting."

C) needed to change their identity to match a common American identity.

D) transcended their humble origins merely by moving to the United States.

6

The phrase "common substance" (line 16) is used to refer to

A) a new, distinctly American cuisine.

B) Crèvecoeur's use of the term "melting pot."

C) a culture and identity shared by all Americans.

D) a unified populace made of many diverse and distinct groups.

Questions 7–8 are based on the following passage.

The goal of plants, or any living organism, is to propagate as much as possible. To this end, many plants in the wild, including wheat's
Line ancestor, have mechanisms that scatter seeds
5 as widely as possible. However, this adaptation makes it difficult to cultivate some plants; it is impossible to farm productively if a crop is spread hither and thither! Wild wheat had a number of other mechanisms that supported its existence
10 in nature but lessened its usefulness in the field. A number of mutations had to take place before wild wheat was a suitable candidate for agriculture. Humans encouraged these mutations by providing a stable environment that favored
15 and nurtured the mutations that would have proven deleterious in the wild.

7

Which choice best summarizes the main idea of the paragraph?

A) Wheat's evolution into a plant that could be farmed productively was shaped by human needs and actions.

B) Wheat is a difficult plant to farm unless a very stable environment is available.

C) The most important mechanism utilized by wild wheat is the means of scattering seeds as widely as possible.

D) All living organisms seek to reproduce as much as possible.

8

Which choice provides the best evidence for the answer to the previous question?

A) Lines 1–2 ("The . . . possible")

B) Lines 2–5 ("To . . . possible")

C) Lines 8–11 ("Wild . . . field")

D) Lines 13–16 ("Humans . . . wild")

Questions 9–10 are based on the following passage.

Perhaps the scientists most excited about reigniting the lunar program are not lunar specialists, but astronomers studying a wide
Line range of subjects. Such scientists would like
5 new missions to install a huge telescope with a diameter of 30 meters on the far side of the moon. Two things that a telescope needs for optimum operation are extreme cold and very little vibration. Temperatures on the moon
10 can be as frigid as 200°C below zero in craters on the dark side. Because there is no seismic activity, the moon is a steady base. Permanent darkness means the telescope can be in constant use. Proponents claim that under
15 these conditions a lunar-based telescope could accomplish as much in seventeen days as the replacement for the Hubble telescope will in ten years of operation.

9

The main idea of the paragraph is most accurately described by which of the following statements?

A) Most astronomers are in favor of reigniting the lunar program.

B) Some scientists believe the moon is an ideal location for a space telescope.

C) New lunar missions could discover important new features of the moon.

D) The new lunar telescope will replace the defunct Hubble telescope.

10

As used in line 2, "reigniting" most nearly means

A) restarting.

B) relighting.

C) ruling.

D) gaining control over.

Questions 11–12 are based on the following passage.

Robert Schumann's orchestral music has been underappreciated and misunderstood for many years by critics and audiences alike. The
Line nineteenth-century virtuoso's works for the
5 piano are acknowledged as brilliant masterworks. However, his large scale orchestral works have always suffered by comparison to those of contemporaries such as Mendelssohn and Brahms. Perhaps this is because Schumann's
10 works should be measured with a different yardstick. His works are often considered poorly orchestrated, but they actually have an unusual aesthetic. He treats the orchestra as he does the piano: one grand instrument with a uniform
15 sound. This is so different from the approach of most composers that, to many, it has seemed like a failing rather than a conscious artistic choice.

11

The author's primary purpose in this paragraph is to

A) praise Schumann for his innovative approach.

B) reassess a portion of Schumann's portfolio.

C) re-evaluate the standing of Mendelssohn and Brahms.

D) examine the influence of Schumann's performances.

12

The author of this passage would most likely attribute the underappreciation of Schumann's orchestral music to

A) the poor orchestration of the works.

B) comparisons of Schumann to the greater genius of Mendelssohn and Brahms.

C) Schumann's failure to make the best use of instruments other than the piano.

D) the difference between Schumann's approach to the orchestra and that of many other composers.

SHORT PASSAGE DRILLS: ANSWERS AND EXPLANATIONS

1. **C** The passage states that it was not until the twentieth century *that Donne really began to be appreciated.* As Jonson was a *seventeenth-century contemporary* of Donne's, the twentieth-century appreciation of Donne's work was in fact hundreds of years after his death. Thus, (C) is well-supported in the passage, which focuses on a major shift in the way Donne's poetry was perceived. Choice (A) is too broad; it doesn't even mention Donne. Choice (B) is too narrow; the passage is not primarily about Jonson and his opinions. Choice (D) is too narrow; the passage states that several factors hindered Donne's contemporaries from fully appreciating him. Choice (C) is the correct answer.

2. **B** Look to eliminate wrong answers. While the passage states that Yeats admired Donne's *psychological intricacies,* there is no evidence that such admiration meant Yeats was not interested in meter and rhythm. Eliminate (A).

    Though T. S. Eliot and Yeats are both mentioned as examples, there's no evidence that their mutual admiration for Donne's work made them *close,* just as there's no evidence that Yeats's admiration made him interested in imitating Donne's technique. Eliminate (C) and (D). Eliot and Yeats are identified as writers in the passage and they are mentioned as examples of people who began to really admire Donne's poetry during the twentieth century when *modern movements* changed attitudes. Thus, (B) is well-supported by the text and is the correct answer.

3. **D** The paragraph provides a lot of information without much analysis or interpretation. Eliminate (A), as the paragraph does not address the issue of crop safety. Eliminate (B), since no *critique* of the process is offered. Eliminate (C), as *opposition to genetically modified foods* is not mentioned, let alone overcome. Choice (D) is consistent with the paragraph's focus on providing information and is the correct answer.

4. **A** Return to the indicated sentence and replace the word *yield* with a word or phrase that makes sense in the context. In this sentence, *yield* must mean something like *make* or *give rise to.* Eliminate (B) and (C) because while both are possible meanings of yield, they do not match the sense needed in the sentence. Eliminate (D), as it also does not match the prediction. Choice (A), *produce,* fits the sense of *make* or *give rise to* and is the correct answer.

5. **C** The *debate* mentioned in line 11 is over what the term *melting* means, and the passage offers two alternatives, one in which *diverse peoples* live together peacefully but keep their differences and another in which those differences are refashioned into a new, shared thing. Eliminate (A), which uses language directly from the passage to say something the passage does not say. Eliminate (B), because the debate was not over whether *immigrant groups understood* the term but over how the term itself was interpreted. Eliminate (D), which also uses language from the passage but does not address the debate described in the relevant sentence. Choice (C) does address the question of the degree to which immigrant groups needed to change their identity and thus is the correct answer.

6. **C** Notice how much easier this question is after you have done the work for question 5, which focused on the debate about whether the term *melting* described *diverse peoples coexisting peacefully while maintaining their differences* or diverse peoples *refashioning themselves to blend indistinguishably into a new, common substance.* This question asks about the phrase *common substance,* which is part of the latter option in the pair. Eliminate (A), as the paragraph does not address the issue of *cuisine.* Eliminate (B), as the *common substance* is part of one way to interpret Crèvecoeur's term, not a reference to his *use* of the term. Eliminate (D) since the *common substance* interpretation of the term *melting pot* is the version in which all Americans blend together, not the one in which groups maintain their distinct identities. Choice (C) correctly identifies the *common substance* as a culture and identity shared by all Americans, creating a blending that erodes distinctions, and is therefore the correct answer.

7. **A** Questions 7 and 8 are a set of specific paired questions, since question 7 indicates that the answer will be found in a particular paragraph (and not potentially from anywhere within the longer passage in which this paragraph is found). The paragraph introduces the goal of all organisms to *propagate as much as possible* and then discusses the limitation of one means of doing that—scattering seeds—and why this made wild wheat a less productive crop for humans. Noting that a number of mutations had to take place for wheat to evolve into a *suitable candidate for agriculture,* the paragraph ends with its main idea: *Humans encouraged these mutations by providing a stable environment that favored and nurtured the mutations that would have proven deleterious in the wild.* Choice (A) restates this idea effectively, so keep it. Eliminate (B), since the main idea is not that wheat is difficult *to farm* without a stable environment, but that such an environment helped it to evolve. Eliminate (C), as the passage states only that scattering seeds is a mechanism that wild wheat utilized, not that it was the most important one. Eliminate (D), since this idea is too general and does not directly address wheat's development. The correct answer is (A).

8. **D** If, when you worked question 7, you underlined the last sentence in the paragraph as providing evidence to support the claim about the main idea, then this question is basically the bonus of a solve-one-get-one-free set of paired questions. Just skim the answer choices to see that (D) clearly indicates the last sentence. Eliminate (A), (B), and (C). Choice (D) is the correct answer.

9. **B** Check the passage to see if *most* astronomers are in favor of reigniting the lunar program and eliminate (A), since no relative number of astronomers is given. Since the passage overall is about astronomers' interest in the building of a lunar telescope, eliminate (C), which does not mention the lunar telescope and mentions finding new features of the moon, not of the other bodies that could be observed from the moon. A replacement for the Hubble telescope is mentioned, but the proponents of a lunar telescope argue that it could accomplish more than a replacement for the Hubble telescope, not that it would *be* a replacement, so eliminate (D). Choice (B) addresses the desire of some scientists for a lunar telescope to further their study of a wide range of subjects; it is the correct answer.

10. **A** In the context of the passage, *reigniting* has to have something to do with sending out new missions, so the word must mean something like *starting up* or *getting working again*. Between (A) and (B), eliminate (B), which is a more literal synonym that does not work as well as (A) in the context of the sentence. Eliminate (C) and (D), as there's no evidence that the astronomers want to seize control of the program, only that they want it to begin sending out missions to the moon again. The correct answer is (A).

11. **B** The paragraph focuses on what the author considers the *underappreciation* of Schumann's orchestral works. Eliminate (C), since the paragraph is about Schumann, not Brahms and Mendelssohn. Eliminate (D), as Schumann's *performances* are not addressed in the passage. The passage is not as much concerned with *praising* Schumann as it is concerned with the issue of why Schumann's orchestral works have not been as highly regarded as his works for the piano. Eliminate (A). Choice (B) is the correct answer.

12. **D** The paragraph notes that Schumann's *works are often considered poorly orchestrated, but they actually have an unusual aesthetic* and further explains that this aesthetic involves treating the orchestra as *one grand instrument with a uniform sound*. Eliminate (A), as there is no evidence the author agrees with those who think the works are poorly orchestrated. Eliminate (B) because, while there is evidence that Schumann was compared to Brahms and Mendelssohn, there is no evidence to support the claim that author believes those two had *greater genius*. Similarly, while there is evidence that the orchestral works were compared to the works for the piano, there is no evidence to support the idea that the author thinks Schumann's unusual aesthetic resulted in a poor use of the orchestra's instruments. Eliminate (C). Choice (D) is supported by the paragraph, since the author credits Schumann's *unusual aesthetic,* which might also be characterized as his approach to orchestra, as the cause of the misunderstanding and underappreciation of Schumann's orchestral works; this is the correct answer.

Predict the Answer and POE: Drill 1

In the passage below, mark the reference window for each question, where appropriate. Then, UNDERLINE (or paraphrase) your predicted answer for each question. Write down the lines you underlined in the space below the question.

The following passage is excerpted from an auto-biographical novel by Maya Angelou and describes an incident from her youth.

One summer afternoon, sweet-milk fresh in my memory, Mrs. Flowers stopped at the Store to buy provisions. Another Negro woman of her
Line health and age would have been expected to carry
5 the paper sacks home in one hand, but Momma said, "Sister Flowers, I'll send Bailey up to your house with these things."

She smiled that slow dragging smile. "Thank you, Mrs. Henderson. I'd prefer Marguerite,
10 though." They gave each other age-group looks.

Momma said, "Well, that's all right then. Sister, go and change your dress. You going to Sister Flowers's."

There was a little path beside the rocky road,
15 and Mrs. Flowers walked in front swinging her arms and picking her way over the stones.

She said, without turning her head, to me, "I hear you're doing very good school work, Marguerite, but that it's all written. The teachers
20 report that they have trouble getting you to talk in class." We passed the triangular farm on our left and the path widened to allow us to walk together. I hung back in the separate unasked and unanswerable questions.
25 "Come and walk along with me, Marguerite." I couldn't have refused even if I wanted to. She pronounced my name so nicely. Or more correctly, she spoke each word with such clarity that I was certain a foreigner who didn't
30 understand English could have understood her.

"Now no one is going to make you talk— possibly no one can. But bear in mind, language is man's way of communicating with his fellow man and it is language alone which separates him
35 from the lower animals." That was a totally new idea to me, and I would need time to think about it.

"Your grandmother says you read a lot. Every chance you get. That's good, but not good enough.
40 Words mean more than what is set down on paper. It takes the human voice to infuse them with the shades of deeper meaning."

She said she was going to give me some books and that I not only must read them, I must read
45 them aloud.

"I'll accept no excuse if you return a book to me that has been badly handled." My imagination boggled at the punishment I would deserve if in fact I did abuse a book of Mrs. Flowers's. Death
50 would be too kind and brief.

The odors in the house surprised me. Somehow I had never connected Mrs. Flowers with food or eating or any other common experience of common people. There must
55 have been an outhouse, too, but my mind never recorded it.

The sweet scent of vanilla had met us as she opened the door.

"I made tea cookies this morning. You see,
60 I had planned to invite you for cookies and lemonade so we could have this little chat."

They were flat round wafers, slightly browned on the edges and butter-yellow in the center. With the cold lemonade they were sufficient
65 for childhood's lifelong diet. Remembering my manners, I took nice little lady-like bites off the edges. She said she had made them expressly for me. So I jammed one whole cake in my mouth and the rough crumbs scratched the insides of my
70 jaws, and if I hadn't had to swallow, it would have been a dream come true.

As I ate she began the first of what we later called "my lessons in living." She said that I must always be intolerant of ignorance but
75 understanding of illiteracy. That some people, unable to go to school, were more educated and even more intelligent than college professors. She encouraged me to listen carefully to what country people called mother wit.

80　When I finished the cookies she brushed off the table and brought a thick, small book from the bookcase. I had read *A Tale of Two Cities* and found it up to my standards as a romantic novel. She opened the first page and I heard poetry for

85　the first time in my life.

　　"It was the best of times and the worst of times . . ."

　　Her voice slid in and curved down through and over the words. She was nearly singing. I

90　wanted to look at the pages. Were they the same that I had read? Or were there notes, music, lined on the pages, as in a hymn book?

　　"How do you like that?"

　　It occurred to me that she expected a

95　response.

　　The sweet vanilla flavor was still on my tongue and her reading was a wonder in my ears. I had to speak.

　　I said, "Yes ma'am." It was the least I could do,

100　but it was the most also.

　　On that first day, I ran down the hill and into the road (few cars ever came along it). I was liked, and what a difference it made. I was respected not as Mrs. Henderson's grandchild or Bailey's sister

105　but for just being Marguerite Johnson.

1.　The narrative point of view of the passage is that of

2.　In the context of the passage, lines 26–30 ("I couldn't . . . her) are primarily meant to

3.　As used in line 42, "shades" most nearly means

4.　In the context of the passage, Marguerite's statement "My imagination boggled at the punishment I would deserve if in fact I did abuse a book of Mrs. Flowers's" (lines 47–49) is primarily meant to convey the idea that

5.　According to Mrs. Flowers, which of the following is a "lesson in living"?

6.　Which choice provides the best evidence for the answer to the previous question?

7.　Marguerite's statement in lines 82–83 ("I had . . . novel") suggests that she initially viewed *A Tale of Two Cities* as

8.　In the context of the passage, Marguerite's question in lines 90–92 ("Were they . . . book") primarily serves to

9.　Marguerite's attitude toward Mrs. Flowers in lines 94–100 ("It occurred . . . also") is best described as one of

10.　According to Mrs. Flowers, which of the following is enhanced by the human voice?

11.　Which choice provides the best evidence for the answer to the previous question?

Now compare each answer choice to your underlined prediction and use POE!

1

The narrative point of view of the passage is that of

A) a woman explaining the importance of reading.

B) a child presenting her opinions on a particular novel.

C) an adult recounting a memorable childhood experience.

D) a writer describing why she chose to write.

2

In the context of the passage, lines 26–30 ("I couldn't . . . her) are primarily meant to

A) recount an anecdote.

B) describe a theory.

C) present an example.

D) note an impression.

3

As used in line 42, "shades" most nearly means

A) shadows.

B) reflections.

C) levels.

D) insights.

4

In the context of the passage, Marguerite's statement "My imagination boggled at the punishment I would deserve if in fact I did abuse a book of Mrs. Flowers's" (lines 47–49) is primarily meant to convey the idea that

A) Mrs. Flowers is known for her strict and unforgiving nature.

B) Mrs. Flowers is overly concerned with the importance of books.

C) Marguerite would fear for her life if she harmed one of Mrs. Flowers's books.

D) Marguerite is unlikely to mistreat one of Mrs. Flowers's books.

5

According to Mrs. Flowers, which of the following is a "lesson in living"?

A) Intelligence is not dependent on formal education.

B) Intellectuals are not as clever as many people suppose.

C) Well-educated people lack common sense.

D) Impoverished people are deserving of compassion.

6

Which choice provides the best evidence for the answer to the previous question?

A) Lines 43–45 ("She said . . . aloud")

B) Lines 65–67 ("Remembering my . . . edges")

C) Lines 73–75 ("She said . . . illiteracy")

D) Lines 75–77 ("That some . . . professors")

Marguerite's statement in lines 82–83 ("I had . . . novel") suggests that she initially viewed *A Tale of Two Cities* as

A) original.

B) sentimental.

C) satisfactory.

D) stunning.

In the context of the passage, Marguerite's question in lines 90–92 ("Were they . . . book") primarily serves to

A) imply that Marguerite was bewildered by Mrs. Flowers's unusual speech patterns.

B) show the religious fervor that Mrs. Flowers brought to her reading.

C) indicate that Mrs. Flowers had set the words of the book to music.

D) convey Marguerite's admiration for the eloquence of Mrs. Flowers's reading.

Marguerite's attitude toward Mrs. Flowers in lines 94–100 ("It occurred . . . also") is best described as one of

A) respectful awe.

B) grudging acceptance.

C) relaxed affection.

D) guarded fear.

According to Mrs. Flowers, the human voice enhances which of the following?

A) Words

B) Poetry

C) Education

D) Freedom

Which choice provides the best evidence for the answer to the previous question?

A) Lines 18–21 ("I hear . . . class")

B) Lines 38–42 ("Your grandmother . . . meaning")

C) Lines 67–71 ("She said . . . true")

D) Lines 101–103 ("On that . . . made")

DRILL 1 REVIEW

1. I was able to predict the answer for _____ questions.
2. Compared to the given answer choices, my predicted answers matched _____ times.
3. TRUE / FALSE: I used POE symbols for all answer choices on all questions.
4. Some new vocabulary words that I need to learn from this passage are as follows:

_____

_____

_____

Predict the Answer and POE: Drill 2

In the passage below, mark the reference window for each question, where appropriate. Then, UNDERLINE (or paraphrase) your predicted answer for each question. Write down the lines you underlined in the space below the question.

The following passage is adapted from a 2010 short story about a woman who comes back to the United States after living for four years in Europe.

By the time I was 22, my girlhood home seemed like the real foreign country, not the language or even the people, but that combination of familiarity and fear. In that combination, I
Line
5   sensed my own closed-mindedness and open-heartedness all at once. I had my way of life, and I'd have to learn a new one to come here.

It's said that you can never really be at home in a foreign country, that your national origins are
10 attached to you like fingerprints. And, of course, when people are conversing easily and fluidly in a language you may never perfect, you're on the outside, and they're on the inside.

I definitely know what it means to be on the
15 outside. I was born and raised in a place that could not be more American, but for those four college years, every time I stepped out of my front door, I could feel myself cycling through thousands of different identities. I belonged here
20 as much as anyone else. Like a local, I could assimilate the collection of odd sights on my walk to school: the homeless man with a different dog every day, the park with shards of classical sculpture, and the former government buildings
25 that now sold American electronics at a huge markup.

I embraced the strangeness, walking down the street with my eyes and ears as open as vast doorways. I embraced the way that leaving my
30 apartment, in pursuit of newspapers in soothing, familiar English or breads so light and fluffy they might've been made from clouds, never felt like entering one foreign country, but like entering many of them, with all the world's cultures and
35 races represented in a panoply of storefronts, restaurants, languages, clothing, and people.

Imagine a rainbow with three times as many colors as it normally has.

But my days on the rainbow were short-lived.
40 It was four years altogether, my four years of college, first in London then in Paris, until my school's commencement, which felt like an ironic name when all I could feel was the end. I came back to Virginia that July, and after months of
45 kicking and screaming that I did not belong here anymore, I couldn't help feeling that I had never left. I both loved and hated this feeling. I felt like a stranger in a very familiar land, as if I had been hired to play a difficult role that only I could play.
50 My jetsetter persona from college would be appalled if she knew that this is what waited for her after her travels. I wanted to make the United States, especially my little corner of Virginia, a fond memory, an object of nostalgia rather than
55 a real home, as I spent the rest of my days in Europe. Instead, here I was in the car with my parents, riding in the passenger seat as I had when I was a teenager, and there they all were, behind every familiar door, every address plaque,
60 every twist and turn of the driveways: all the people that I knew from my youth were here and looked oddly the same, but I looked like them, too.

"How does it feel to come back?" asked my
65 father, and after a moment of consideration (a long moment, for my father is never in a hurry), I knew that "come back" had different meanings for the two of us. For him, it was "back home," the place that he and I would always return to,
70 but for me it was "back in time," as I had always imagined my future to be on the other side of the Atlantic Ocean.

My hometown—for that much it surely is—lies just to the west of the Shenandoah Valley.
75 The town is tiny, maybe 500 people altogether, but I learned on our drive back from the airport in Washington, D.C., that my "hometown" has much more capacious borders than I had ever realized. The majestic Shenandoahs tower above
80 the scenery, and you can take them in from many

miles away. Once you leave the D.C. suburbs in Virginia, you can feel the warmth of communities that historically had only their own resources on which to rely. Every trip here was a trip "back"
85 as only a few technological updates made secret changes within a visually unchanged landscape. I was coming back not only to my own home but also to the homes of many others before me.

I wanted to be like all my favorite American
90 expatriates from the 1920s, and maybe I could have been. But my circumstances brought me back here. I should consider it a great privilege rather than an insufferable burden that I had nothing to escape from, so why pretend
95 otherwise? I could've made it in Paris, I think, but now, I finally realize that I can just as well make it here, too. I didn't have to be a foreigner to feel like myself. This community doesn't have to swallow everything that makes me an individual. It can
100 take me in, and in fact, it can give me the freedom to be myself in a way that the hustle and bustle, the true unfamiliarity, of Paris and London never could. At home, I can be a local or a stranger as I please.

12. The central contrast in the passage is between

13. In the passage, the narrator is concerned primarily with

14. As it is used in line 10, the word "fingerprints" is a simile for

15. Lines 22–26 ("the homeless . . . markup") are similar to lines 59–60 ("every familiar . . . driveways") in the way they

16. In context, the phrase "my days on the rainbow" (line 39) refers mainly to a time that the narrator was

17. Which choice provides the best evidence for the answer to the previous question?

18. Lines 47–49 ("I both . . . play") are notable for their description of

19. In line 58, the word "they" refers to

20. In line 85, "secret" most nearly means

21. The narrator's description of the "warmth" (line 82) chiefly reveals her

22. In lines 92–95 ("I should . . . otherwise"), the narrator poses a question that primarily

Now compare each answer choice to your underlined prediction and use POE!

12

The central contrast in the passage is between

A) anger and redemption.

B) foreignness and sophistication.

C) maturity and childishness.

D) familiarity and unfamiliarity.

13

In the passage, the narrator is concerned primarily with

A) extending a heated disagreement with her parents.

B) settling reluctantly into a shocking new reality.

C) reminiscing about the most difficult period of her life.

D) characterizing her acceptance of a change in life.

14

As it is used in line 10, the word "fingerprints" is a simile for

A) manual labor.

B) criminal proceedings.

C) inescapable marks.

D) celebratory gestures.

15

Lines 22–26 ("the homeless . . . markup") are similar to lines 59–60 ("every familiar . . . driveways") in the way they

A) correct a misrecognition.

B) create a fantastic setting.

C) describe a scene.

D) evoke a paradox.

16

In context, the phrase "my days on the rainbow" (line 39) refers mainly to a time that the narrator was

A) living a pleasantly varied and diverse lifestyle.

B) often flying back and forth between continents.

C) denying the natural beauty of her home state.

D) ignoring her studies for extracurricular activities.

17

Which choice provides the best evidence for the answer to the previous question?

A) Lines 37–38 ("Imagine a . . . has")

B) Line 39 ("But my . . . short-lived")

C) Lines 43–47 ("I came . . . left")

D) Lines 47–49 ("I felt . . . play")

18

Lines 47–49 ("I both . . . play") are notable for their description of

A) unscrupulous actions.

B) theatrical performances.

C) deep-seated antipathies.

D) conflicted feelings.

19

In line 58, the word "they" refers to

A) "travels" (line 52).

B) "days" (line 55).

C) "driveways" (line 60).

D) "people" (line 61).

In line 85, "secret" most nearly means

A) unspoken.

B) invisible.

C) embarrassing.

D) shameful.

The narrator's description of the "warmth" (line 82) chiefly reveals her

A) anger.

B) comfort.

C) foreignness.

D) age.

In lines 92–95 ("I should . . . otherwise"), the narrator poses a question that primarily

A) shows her defensive stance.

B) argues for an older way of life.

C) demonstrates her calm acceptance.

D) evokes her international experience.

DRILL 2 REVIEW

1. I was able to predict the answer for _____ questions.
2. Compared to the given answer choices, my predicted answers matched _____ times.
3. TRUE / FALSE: I used POE symbols for all answer choices on all questions.
4. Some new vocabulary words that I need to learn from this passage are as follows:

_____

_____

_____

Predict the Answer and POE: Drill 3

In the passage below, mark the reference window for each question, where appropriate. Then, UNDERLINE (or paraphrase) your predicted answer for each question. Write down the lines you underlined in the space below the question.

The following passage is adapted from Edith Wharton's *The House of Mirth,* a novel set in the early twentieth century. Lily Bart, a New York socialite, is speaking with her friend Lawrence Selden about some of the differences between the lives led by women and men.

Lily sank with a sigh into one of the shabby leather chairs.

"How delicious to have a place like this all to one's self! What a miserable thing it is to
5 be a woman." She leaned back in a luxury of discontent.

Selden was rummaging in a cupboard for the cake.

"Even women," he said, "have been known to
10 enjoy the privileges of a flat."

"Oh, governesses—or widows. But not girls—not poor, miserable, marriageable girls!"

"I even know a girl who lives in a flat."

She sat up in surprise. "You do?"
15 "I do," he assured her, emerging from the cupboard with the sought-for cake.

"Oh, I know—you mean Gerty Farish." She smiled a little unkindly. "But I said marriageable—and besides, she has a horrid little
20 place, and no maid, and such odd things to eat. Her cook does the washing and the food tastes of soap. I should hate that, you know."

She began to saunter about the room, examining the bookshelves. Suddenly her
25 expression changed from desultory enjoyment to active conjecture, and she turned to Selden with a question. "You collect, don't you—you know about first editions and things?"

He had seated himself on an arm of the chair
30 near which she was standing, and she continued to question him, asking which were the rarest volumes, whether the Jefferson Gryce collection was really considered the finest in the world, and what was the largest price ever fetched by a single
35 volume.

It was so pleasant to sit there looking up at her, as she lifted now one book and then another from the shelves, fluttering the pages between her fingers, while her drooping profile was outlined
40 against the warm background of old bindings, that he talked on without pausing to wonder at her sudden interest in so unsuggestive a subject. But he could never be long with her without trying to find a reason for what she was doing,
45 and as she replaced his first edition of *La Bruyère* and turned away from the bookcases, he began to ask himself what she had been driving at. Her next question was not of a nature to enlighten him. She paused before him with a smile which
50 seemed at once designed to admit him to her familiarity, and to remind him of the restrictions it imposed.

"Don't you ever mind," she asked suddenly, "not being rich enough to buy all the books you
55 want?"

He followed her glance about the room, with its worn furniture and shabby walls.

"Don't I just? Do you take me for a saint on a pillar?"
60 "And having to work—do you mind that?"

"Oh, the work itself is not so bad—I'm rather fond of the law."

"No; but the being tied down: the routine—don't you ever want to get away, to see new places
65 and people?"

"Horribly—especially when I see all my friends rushing to the steamer."

She drew a sympathetic breath. "But do you mind enough—to marry to get out of it?"
70 Selden broke into a laugh. "God forbid!" he declared.

She rose with a sigh.

"Ah, there's the difference—a girl must, a man may if he chooses." She surveyed him critically.
75 "Your coat's a little shabby—but who cares? It doesn't keep people from asking you to dine. If I were shabby no one would have me: a woman is

asked out as much for her clothes as for herself. The clothes are the background, the frame, if
80 you like: they don't make success, but they are a part of it. Who wants a dingy woman? We are expected to be pretty and well-dressed till we drop—and if we can't keep it up alone, we have to go into partnership."
85   Selden glanced at her with amusement: it was impossible, even with her lovely eyes imploring him, to take a sentimental view of her case.
        "Ah, well, there must be plenty of capital on the look-out for such an investment. Perhaps
90 you'll meet your fate tonight at the Trenors."

23.   Lily's tone at the beginning of the pas-sage is one of

24.   Which choice provides the best evidence for the answer to the previous question?

25.   In line 11 ("Oh, governesses—or wid-ows"), Lily's comment serves to

26.   Lily's remarks in lines 17–22 ("Oh,...you know") help to convey her

27.   In lines 43–49 ("But he...him"), Selden is best described as

28.   In line 50, "designed" most nearly means

29.   Selden's response to Lily in lines 58–59 ("Don't I...pillar") most directly suggests that he

30.   Lily's observation in line 75 ("Your coat's...cares") serves primarily to

31.   Lily's remarks about marriage primarily indicate that she views marriage as a

32.   In line 87, "sentimental" most nearly means

33.   In line 90, Selden's use of the word "fate" refers to the

Now compare each answer choice to your underlined prediction and use POE!

23

Lily's tone at the beginning of the passage is one of

A) surprise.

B) indignation.

C) delight.

D) self-pity.

24

Which choice provides the best evidence for the answer to the previous question?

A) Lines 3–4 ("How delicious . . . self")

B) Lines 4–5 ("What a . . . woman")

C) Line 14 ("She sat . . . surprise")

D) Lines 23–24 (She began . . . bookshelves")

25

In line 11 ("Oh, governesses—or widows"), Lily's comment serves to

A) express anger about a change in social status.

B) bemoan the lack of help in Selden's apartment.

C) call attention to a person's arrogant behavior.

D) indicate exceptions to a perceived rule.

26

Lily's remarks in lines 17–22 ("Oh, . . . you know") help to convey her

A) dislike of a former friend.

B) distaste for a certain lifestyle.

C) fear of an uncertain future.

D) concern for a close friend.

27

In lines 43–49 ("But he . . . him"), Selden is best described as

A) irritated by Lily's childish questions about literature.

B) puzzled by Lily's fascination with financial matters.

C) disturbed by Lily's casual treatment of his book collection.

D) uncertain about the motivation for Lily's actions.

28

In line 50, "designed" most nearly means

A) renovated.

B) charted.

C) intended.

D) allowed.

29

Selden's response to Lily in lines 58–59 ("Don't I . . . pillar") most directly suggests that he

A) regrets his decision to become a lawyer.

B) wishes to be seen as deeply religious.

C) hopes to move to a wealthier neighborhood.

D) agrees that wealth has certain advantages.

30

Lily's observation in line 75 ("Your coat's . . . cares") serves primarily to

A) ridicule a character.

B) dismiss a belief.

C) highlight a discrepancy.

D) voice a concern.

Lily's remarks in the passage indicate that she views marriage as a

A) natural result of a prolonged courtship.

B) happy coincidence that cannot be counted on.

C) distant dream for the average person.

D) practical necessity for a young woman.

In line 87, "sentimental" most nearly means

A) melodramatic.

B) nostalgic.

C) sympathetic.

D) subjective.

In line 90, Selden's use of the word "fate" refers to the

A) possibility that Lily will meet a potential suitor.

B) likelihood that Lily will be forced to remain single.

C) conviction that people's lives are largely predetermined.

D) probability that a business venture will be profitable.

DRILL 3 REVIEW

1. I was able to predict the answer for _____ questions.
2. Compared to the given answer choices, my predicted answers matched _____ times.
3. TRUE / FALSE: I used POE symbols for all answer choices on all questions.
4. Some new vocabulary words that I need to learn from this passage are as follows:

_____

_____

_____

Predict the Answer and POE: Drill 4

In the passage below, mark the reference window for each question, where appropriate. Then, UNDERLINE (or paraphrase) your predicted answer for each question. Write down the lines you underlined in the space below the question.

The following is an adaptation of an essay published by a journalist in a collection of essays on the cultural history of newspapers.

There was a time when journalists were rogue heroes who showed society's hidden workings and did so fearlessly. While the rogue journalist
Line may still exist, our own news-media landscape
5 has altered, and we are necessarily much worse-informed because of it. Particularly on television news, the copywriters have all become editors. That is to say, those who were previously tasked with dredging up the cold, hard facts
10 are now much more likely to provide viewers with predetermined opinions and personal perspectives.

One possible cause for this shift is the increasingly vicious fight for viewers and readers.
15 Not only are there hundreds of channels on the television, there are now literally millions of attention-grabbing options on computers, tablets, and smartphones. After a long, hard day at the office, the average viewer wants an easy time
20 at home, not a mental challenge (life provides enough of those) but a comfortable retelling of the day's events. That retelling can be made most comfortable when it is delivered in an entertaining package by people whose view of the
25 world will basically square with the viewer's own.

A crucial historical example offers the comforting reminder that things were not always this way. Joseph Pulitzer was born in Mako, Hungary, in 1847. In his younger years, Pulitzer
30 wanted to be a soldier. He was turned away from the Austrian Army, but in Germany, he was eventually recruited to fight as a mercenary in the U.S. Union Army. After the Civil War ended, Pulitzer made his way to St. Louis, where he
35 began to study English and law. A chance meeting with two German newspaper owners led to Pulitzer's first job as a copywriter.

Pulitzer was a tireless and innovative journalist. He worked doggedly to write high-quality stories and to increase the circulation of
40 his papers. At the shockingly young age of 31, Pulitzer was the owner of the English-language St. Louis *Post-Dispatch,* where he oversaw all aspects of the newspaper's publication. In this
45 era, Pulitzer became particularly interested in championing the causes of the common man. His paper commonly featured exposes of the corruption of the rich and powerful. Circulation of the *Post-Dispatch* rose to such heights, in
50 fact, that Pulitzer was able to purchase the much larger *New York World* in 1883. Pulitzer's same commitment to exposing corruption and educating his underrepresented public created what has been called a "one-man revolution" in
55 the World's editorial policies and in newspaper publishing more generally.

One of the most vicious circulation battles of Pulitzer's career came from 1896 to 1898, the period of the Spanish-American War. This
60 war famously stretched the limits of journalistic objectivity, and Pulitzer's main competitor, William Randolph Hearst, famously said to one of his photographers, "You supply the pictures, and I'll supply the war." In the context of Pulitzer's
65 larger career, it is especially unfortunate that Pulitzer was equally guilty of these kinds of fabrications, though the battle soured him on this kind of sensationalist journalism for the remainder of his career.

70 With Hearst at the forefront of this new "yellow journalism," newspapers became the mouthpieces for the ideologies of their editors, not for the hard realities of common men. Pulitzer withdrew from this method of
75 journalism, and in time, the *New York World* became a more nuanced newspaper. With the paper's help and at its prodding, the U.S. government protected American business by passing new antitrust legislation and by

80 regulating an increasingly out-of-control insurance industry.

Pulitzer's name is best-known today because of its association with the Pulitzer Prize, awarded every year to works ranging from journalism to
85 drama. The prize, especially the prize awarded for journalism, serves as a constant reminder that journalism is most valuable when it is at its most honest. Pulitzer explained his journalistic credo this way: "An able, disinterested, public-
90 spirited press, with trained intelligence to know the right and courage to do it, can preserve that public virtue without which popular government is a sham and a mockery." He would surely be disappointed in the direction that journalism has
95 taken today, and we should be, too. We can only hold out the hope that someone with Pulitzer's courage and perseverance can come along to restore journalism to its rightful place as teller of things as they really are. Only then can we begin
100 to change those things to how they really should be.

34. The primary purpose of the passage is to

35. The author's attitude toward the journalists described in the first paragraph is best characterized as

36. Which choice provides the best evidence for the answer to the previous question?

37. The information in lines 28–37 ("Joseph Pulitzer . . . copywriter") serves primarily to

38. The information in lines 41–44 ("At the . . . publication") reveals Pulitzer's

39. The misfortune referred to in lines 64–69 ("In the . . . career") is that

40. The author's comment in lines 93–95 ("He would . . . too") is best described as

41. The "hope" referred to in line 96 is that

42. Which of the following, if true, is the author most likely to see as an unfortunate consequence of modern journalistic practices?

43. Which choice provides the best evidence for the answer to the previous question?

Now compare each answer choice to your underlined prediction and use POE!

34

The primary purpose of the passage is to

A) detail the contributions of immigrants to contemporary journalism.

B) garner support for the return of print in place of electronic media.

C) blame the reading public for its lack of interest in current events.

D) draw the reader's attention to an issue in contemporary news reporting.

35

The author's attitude toward the journalists described in the first paragraph is best characterized as

A) confused.

B) obstinate.

C) open-minded.

D) disapproving.

36

Which phrase provides the best evidence for the answer to the previous question?

A) Lines 1–3 ("There was . . . fearlessly")

B) Lines 3–6 ("While the . . . it")

C) Lines 6–7 ("Particularly on . . . editors")

D) Lines 8–12 ("That is . . . perspectives")

37

The information in lines 28–37 ("Joseph Pulitzer . . . copywriter") serves primarily to

A) explain the reasons behind Pulitzer's change in career.

B) sketch the early career of a historical figure.

C) preview the conflicts outlined in the following paragraph.

D) decry the state of contemporary journalism and media.

38

The information in lines 41–44 ("At the . . . publication") reveals Pulitzer's

A) apathy.

B) humbleness.

C) kindness.

D) precociousness.

39

The misfortune referred to in lines 64–69 ("In the . . . career") is that

A) Pulitzer stopped competing with Hearst for readers and lost the circulation battle.

B) Pulitzer built the remainder of his career on a series of dubious journalistic practices.

C) a career built on journalistic integrity should be compromised by this particular lapse.

D) many journalists used sensationalist tactics to gain an edge in circulation.

40

The author's comment in lines 93–95 ("He would . . . too") is best described as

A) an overstatement.

B) a critique.

C) a hypothesis.

D) a concession.

The "hope" referred to in line 96 is that

A) journalists will stop listening to the corporate interests of their editors.

B) a brave individual will come along and change the face of journalism forever.

C) news reporting will free itself from sensationalism and return to an era of purer objectivity.

D) journalistic integrity will be recognized as the true way to produce social change.

Which of the following, if true, is the author most likely to see as an unfortunate consequence of modern journalistic practices?

A) A rural journalist accepts a higher salary to transfer to a popular newspaper published in an urban area.

B) A newspaper editor is reluctant to state his political views because he fears doing so may decrease the popularity of his paper.

C) A newspaper receives public scrutiny for uncovering the details of corruption within a state government.

D) A television news station that claims to be fair to all political ideologies represents the viewpoints of only one political perspective.

Which choice provides the best evidence for the answer to the previous question?

A) Lines 8–12 ("That is . . . perspectives")

B) Lines 41–44 ("At the . . . publication")

C) Lines 64–69 ("In the . . . career")

D) Lines 93–95 ("He would . . . too")

DRILL 4 REVIEW

1. I was able to predict the answer for _____ questions.
2. Compared to the given answer choices, my predicted answers matched _____ times.
3. TRUE / FALSE: I used POE symbols for all answer choices on all questions.
4. Some new vocabulary words that I need to learn from this passage are as follows:

_____

_____

_____

PREDICT AND POE: ANSWERS AND EXPLANATIONS

Drill 1

1. **C** The question asks for the narrative point of view, which means that the correct choice will refer to what the author's perspective is for the entire passage. General questions such as this should be done after all of the specific questions; also be sure to check the blurb, which indicates that *The following passage is excerpted from an autobiographical novel by Maya Angelou and describes an incident from her youth.* Based on the blurb, the correct answer will say something about an adult woman remembering a childhood memory. Choice (A) matches *Maya Angelou*, but the perspective is not one that explains *the importance of reading,* so eliminate (A). Choice (B) says the point of view is a child's, which is incorrect; eliminate (B). Choice (D) accurately describes Ms. Angelou, but the passage does not explain *why she chose to write,* so eliminate (D). Choice (C) is the correct answer.

2. **D** Context questions ask why an author used a specific word or phrase. Return to the passage and read the necessary window around lines 26–30 to predict the correct answer. From the phrase *she pronounced my name so nicely. Or more correctly, she spoke each word with such clarity,* it can be predicted that the author intended to show the reader how impressed Marguerite was by how Mrs. Flowers spoke. The phrase in question involves neither *a theory* nor *an example,* so eliminate (B) and (C). Marguerite is neither retelling nor recounting a story or anecdote; eliminate (A). The author does share Marguerite's *impression* with the reader within lines 26–30. Choice (D) is the correct answer.

3. **C** The question asks what *shades most nearly* means, so this is a Vocab-in-Context question. Remember to cross out the word in quotation marks and substitute an alternative word. Then, rely on Process of Elimination. In this case *degrees* would be a good synonym to explain how *deeper meaning* was being infused by the voice. Of the answer choices, only *levels* has a similar meaning to the prediction *degrees.* Choice (C) is the correct answer.

4. **D** Context questions ask why an author used a specific word or phrase. Return to the passage and read the necessary window around lines 47–49 to predict the correct answer. Since Marguerite is the main subject of this paragraph, you can predict that the answer will be referring to her, so eliminate (A) and (B), which talk about Mrs. Flowers. The key phrase required to choose between the remaining options (C) and (D) comes in the sentence after the quoted phrase: *Death would be too kind and brief.* Since this is an autobiography, it can be predicted that the author was being hyperbolic to show the reader how much she did not want to return a book that *has been badly handled.* Choice (D) is the correct answer.

5. **A** Note that the following question is a best evidence question, so this question and Q6 can be answered in tandem. Detail questions ask for information regarding a key word or line reference. In this case there is no line reference for Q5, but by skimming for the lead words *lesson in living,* it can be determined that the evidence will be around line 68. Look at the answers for Q6 first. The lines

in (6A) and (6B) are outside the window, so eliminate both. *She said that I must always be intolerant of ignorance but understanding of illiteracy* is within the window, so look to see if those words support any of the answers in Q5. None of the Q5 choices refer to illiteracy or ignorance, so (6C) can be eliminated. Now evaluate (6D) which says *That some people, unable to go to school, were more educated and even more intelligent than college professors.* From this, it can be predicted that a *lesson in living* could be that some people who did not go to school were smarter than some that went to college. Choice (5A) accurately matches this prediction, so keep it. Choice (5B) questions the cleverness of intellectuals, but Mrs. Flowers mentions only those *unable to go to school;* she does not attack the intelligence of intellectuals; eliminate (5B). Choice (5C) may be eliminated for the same reason. *Impoverished people* are not mentioned, so eliminate (5D). Choices (5A) and (6D) are the correct answers.

6. **D** (See explanation above)

7. **C** The question asks how Marguerite initially viewed *A Tale of Two Cities.* Line 83 indicates that she *found it up to (her) standards,* so the prediction could simply be "of sufficient quality." Because *original, sentimental,* and *stunning* do not match this prediction, eliminate (A), (B), and (D). Choice (C) is the correct answer.

8. **D** Context questions ask why an author used a specific word or phrase. Return to the passage and read the necessary window before lines 90–92 to predict the correct answer. Marguerite is listening to Mrs. Flowers read *A Tale of Two Cities* in this section, so it can be predicted that the answer will be referring to Marguerite listening to Mrs. Flowers. Marguerite does not find any patterns unusual, so eliminate (A). Marguerite's reference to a *hymn book* illustrates how melodic the reading was, not that it was literally set to music, nor that *religious fervor* played any role; eliminate (B) and (C). Choice (D) is the correct answer.

9. **A** Attitude questions ask how an author or character feels regarding something in a passage—in this case how Marguerite feels about Mrs. Flowers. From reading the window of lines 94–100, specifically *her reading was a wonder in my ears,* it can be predicted that Marguerite was impressed. Only *respectful awe* captures this sentiment. Choice (A) is the correct answer.

10. **A** Note that the following question is a best evidence question, so this question and Q11 can be answered in tandem. Detail questions ask for information regarding a key word or line reference. In this case there is no line reference for Q10, but by skimming for the lead words *human voice,* it can be determined that the evidence will be around line 38. Look at the answers for Q11 first. Only answer (11B) is even close to the reference window found by skimming for the words *human voice,* so evaluate this choice first. Q10 asks what is enhanced by the human voice and according to the excerpt in (11B), words are infused by *the human voice* with *shades of deeper meaning,* which matches (10A). Nowhere in the passage are *poetry, education, or freedom* mentioned in tandem with *the human voice,* so eliminate (10B), (10C), and (10D). Choices (10A) and (11B) are the correct answers.

11. **B** (See explanation above)

Vocab Check

Here is a list of challenging words from Drill 1. If you don't know the definitions, look them up to learn them!

impoverished   anecdote   incomprehensible   eloquence   fervor   sentimental

Drill 2

12. **D** General questions such as this should be done after all of the specific questions. Also be sure to check the blurb, which indicates that *The following passage is adapted from a 2010 short story about a woman who comes back to the United States after living for four years in Europe*. This blurb does not provide enough information to make much of a prediction, so this question should be left for last. After reading the passage and completing all of the specific questions, it becomes clear that the prediction concerning the central contrast could be something similar to what the author knows and what she doesn't. There is no reference to the author's *anger* or *maturity*, so eliminate (A) and (C). Choice (B) references the *foreignness* that the author feels, but she finds foreign places to be sophisticated, so eliminate (B). *Familiarity and unfamiliarity* match the prediction. Choice (D) is the correct answer.

13. **D** General questions such as this should be done after all of the specific questions. Then, it becomes clear that the narrator is concerned with accepting changes in her life. Words such as *heated disagreement*, *shocking*, and *most difficult* are too extreme to be supported by the passage; eliminate (A), (B), and (C). Choice (D) is the correct answer.

14. **C** The question asks what *fingerprints is a simile for*, so this is a Vocab-in-Context question. Remember to cross out the word in quotation marks and substitute an alternative word. Then, use POE. In this case *ink stains* would be a good synonym to explain the phrase *attached to you like fingerprints*. Of the answer choices, only *inescapable marks* would share characteristics with the prediction. Choice (C) is the correct answer.

15. **C** The question asks how the two phrases are similar, so read the reference windows and provide a prediction of how they are similar. In this case they both provide a description of what the narrator sees. These scenes are not a *misrecognition*, *a fantastic setting*, or *a paradox*, so eliminate (A), (B), and (D). Choice (C) is the correct answer.

16. **A** Note that the following question is a best evidence question, so this question and Q17 can be answered in tandem. Context questions ask why an author used a specific word or phrase. Return to the passage and read the necessary window around line 39 to predict the correct answer. From the two sentences before the phrase referenced in Q16, it can be predicted that the narrator believed that her experience was positively diverse. Look at the answers for Q16 first. Choice (17B) is the phrase from Q16 itself, so eliminate (17B). Lines 40–49 are negative in tone; eliminate (17C) and (17D). Only answer (17A) captures the positive tone of the prediction. Return to Q16 and seek

an answer that is equally positive. Choice (16A) also matches the tone of the prediction. Choices (16A) and (17A) are the correct answers.

17. **A** (See explanation above)

18. **D** The question asks for a detail regarding the description provided in lines 47–49, so read the reference window to make a prediction. The window indicates that the narrator was providing a scene to show how she was conflicted because she *both loved and hated this feeling*. Only (D) provides an accurate portrayal of this conflict. Choice (D) is the correct answer.

19. **D** The question asks what "they" *refers to*, so this is a context question. Context questions ask why an author used a specific word or phrase. The colon in the sentence is a good clue. After that point in the sentence, it can be predicted that the narrator is referring to *all the people that (she) knew*. Choice (D) is the correct answer.

20. **B** The question asks what "secret" *means*, so this is a Vocab-in-Context question. Remember to cross out the word in quotation marks and substitute an alternative word. Then, use POE. In lines 85–86 it is clear that these *secret changes* exist *within a visually unchanged landscape*. The choices *unspoken*, *embarrassing*, and *shameful* do not match *visually unchanged*. Choice (B) is the correct answer.

21. **B** The question asks what the word *warmth* reveals about the author, so this is a context question. Context questions ask why an author used a specific word or phrase. The overall tone in this paragraph, as with the passage as a whole, is positive. Therefore, warmth is a positive term. The words *anger*, *foreignness*, and *age* are not even marginally positive terms; eliminate (A), (C), and (D). Choice (B) is the correct answer.

22. **C** The question asks why the author poses the question in lines 92–95, so this is a context question. Context questions ask why an author used a specific word or phrase. The narrator answers the question *I should consider it a great privilege rather than an insufferable burden that I had nothing to escape from, so why pretend otherwise?* by asserting that she *could've made it in Paris,* but she *can just as well make it here, too.* This shows that she accepts how her life has played out; she is not *defensive* and it cannot be said that she *argues*, so eliminate (A) and (B). While Paris involved an *international experience,* she does not ask the question to evoke this experience, so eliminate (D). Choice (C) is the correct answer.

Vocab Check

Here is a list of challenging words from Drill 2. If you don't know the definitions, look them up to learn them!

paradox   irony   allusion   singularity   unscrupulous   antipathy

Drill 3

23. **D** Note that the following question is a best evidence question, so this question and Q23 can be answered in tandem. This question asks about *Lily's tone*. For specific detail questions without a line reference, find the reference window based on lead words and make a prediction based on what is supported by the passage. From the phrase *Lily sank with a sigh*, which begins the passage, through Lily saying *poor, miserable, marriageable girls* in line 12, it is shown that *Lily's tone* is an unhappy one. Look at the answers for Q24 first: two are outside of the reference window, so eliminate (24C) and (24D). Choice (24A) references *How delicious to have a place like this all to one's self*, while *What a miserable thing it is to be a woman* captures the unhappy tone predicted. Return to Q23 and find an answer that matches this negativity. Neither *surprise* nor *delight* match *unhappy*; eliminate (23A) and (23C). Choice (23B) *indignation* is negative, but connotes anger, whereas Lily is more *miserable* and sunken, so eliminate (23B). Choices (23D) and (24B) are the correct answers.

24. **B** (See explanation above)

25. **D** The question asks what *Lily's comment serves to* do in line 11, so this is a context question. Context questions ask why an author used a specific word or phrase. Lily's comment *Oh, governesses—or widows. But not girls—not poor, miserable, marriageable girls* is made to counter Selden's comment that *women have been known to enjoy the privileges of a flat*, so it can be predicted that her response was to counteract a position. Lily's statement is made in response to Selden's comment, not anything about Selden himself, so eliminate (B) and (C). Lily references social status, but hers has not changed; eliminate (A). Indicating *exceptions* is a way to counter a statement. Choice (D) is the correct answer.

26. **B** The question asks what *Lily's remarks* in lines 17–22 convey, so this is a context question. Context questions ask why an author used a specific word or phrase. Lily's comment *she has a horrid little place, and no maid, and such odd things to eat... I should hate that, you know* shows that Lily dislikes how Gerty Farish lives, so a good prediction will match this information. Lily's main point was not personally about Gerty Farish, so eliminate (A) and (D). Lily is not discussing her future in this sentence; eliminate (C). Choice (B) is the correct answer.

27. **D** The question asks for specific details about how Selden is described, so read the reference window to make a prediction. In line 47 Selden asks *himself what she had been driving at*, so an accurate prediction will deal with him having questions about Lily. Selden is questioning of Lily, but he is neither *irritated* nor *disturbed* by her; eliminate (A) and (C). Choice (B) accurately identifies Selden as *puzzled*, but this is not regarding *Lily's fascination with financial matters*. Choice (D) is the correct answer.

28. **C** The question asks what "designed" *most nearly* means, so this is a Vocab-in-Context question. Remember to cross out the word in quotation marks and substitute an alternative word. Then, use POE. In this case *meant* would be a good replacement word. Of the answer choices, only *intended* has a similar meaning to the prediction *meant*. Choice (C) is the correct answer.

29. **D** The question asks what *Selden's response* in lines 58–59 *most directly suggests*, so this is a context question. Context questions ask why an author used a specific word or phrase. Selden's comment *Don't I just? Do you take me for a saint on a pillar?* is in direct response to Lily's question *Don't you ever mind not being rich enough to buy all the books you want?* It can therefore be predicted that Selden's negative response means he does in fact mind not being rich enough, which means that for him *wealth has certain advantages*. While Selden might not mind being rich, there is no reference to him desiring a new *wealthier neighborhood*; eliminate (C). There is no mention of Selden's religion or occupation, so eliminate (A) and (B). Choice (D) is the correct answer.

30. **C** The question asks about what *Lily's observation* in line 75 *serves* to do, so this is a context question. Context questions ask why an author used a specific word or phrase. Lily's comment *Your coat's a little shabby—but who cares?* directly follows Lily's claim that a man may choose to marry, but *a girl must*. It can be predicted Lily brought up the coat to highlight this difference between a man and a girl. Both *ridicule* and *dismiss* are the opposite of this prediction, so eliminate (A) and (B). Lily is concerned with her current state of affairs, but this specific observation is not related to her concerns; eliminate (D). The word *discrepancy* means difference. Choice (C) is the correct answer.

31. **D** The question asks about Lily's view of marriage in the passage. By completing the other specific detail questions first, it is easier to complete this general question. Line 73 also lends a prediction that Lily believes *a girl must* marry, which means it is a *practical necessity*, as indicated in (D). It is clear throughout the passage that Lily has a negative opinion of marriage and regards it neither as a *happy coincidence* nor a *dream*, so eliminate (B) and (C). Lily never mentions a *prolonged courtship*; eliminate (A). Choice (D) is the correct answer.

32. **C** The question asks what *sentimental most nearly means*, so this is a Vocab-in-Context question. Remember to cross out the word in quotation marks and substitute an alternative word. Then, use POE. In this case, based on the phrase *her lovely eyes,* the word *lovingly* would be a good replacement. Of the answer choices, only *sympathetic* has a similar meaning to the prediction *lovingly*. Choice (C) is the correct answer.

33. **A** The question asks what *fate refers to*, so this is a Vocab-in-Context question. Remember to cross out the word in quotation marks and substitute an alternative word. Then, use POE. Throughout the passage Lily is talking about her marriage prospects, so it could be predicted that she is seeking her *future husband*. There is nothing to indicate it is likely Lily *will be forced to remain single* or *that people's lives are largely predetermined*, so eliminate (B) and (C). Choice (D) is a trap answer, but there is no indication that Lily is actually a businesswoman. Only (A) matches the prediction. Choice (A) is the correct answer.

Vocab Check

Here is a list of challenging words from Drill 3. If you don't know the definitions, look them up to learn them!

indignation   discrepancy   melodramatic   nostalgic   subjective

Drill 4

34. **D** The question asks for *the primary purpose of the passage*, so this is a general question. General questions such as this should be done after all of the specific questions, but also be sure to check the blurb, which indicates that *The following is an adaptation of an essay published by a journalist in a collection of essays on the cultural history of newspapers.* Based on the blurb, the prediction should say something about *the history of newspapers.* The passage neither argues for the return of print nor blames the reading public for anything, so eliminate (B) and (C). While Pulitzer was an immigrant, there is no discussing the *contributions of immigrants to contemporary journalism*; eliminate (A). Choice (D) is the correct answer.

35. **D** Note that the following question is a best evidence question, so this question and Q36 can be answered in tandem. This question asks about *The author's attitude toward journalists.* For detail questions, find the reference window based on lead words and make a prediction based on what is supported by the passage. The author yearns for *a time when journalists were rogue heroes*, so the prediction should be a negative one. Look at the answers for Q36 first. The opening three sentences describe the change that has occurred in the news business, not how the author feels about this change; eliminate (36A), (36B), and (36C). In the concluding sentence of the opening paragraph, the author prefers *those who were previously tasked with dredging up the cold, hard facts* over today's journalists who *are now much more likely to provide viewers with predetermined opinions and personal perspectives.* Return to Q35 and find an answer that matches this preference for the old over the new. Because *confused, obstinate,* and *open-minded* do not match this preference, eliminate (36A), (36B), and (36C). Choice (36D), *disapproving,* reflects the author's preference for how journalists used to be. Choices (35D) and (36D) are the correct answers.

36. **D** (See explanation above)

37. **B** The question asks about what the biographical information about Joseph Pulitzer in lines 28–37 *serves primarily* to do, so this is a context question. Context questions ask why an author used a specific word or phrase. It can be predicted from the phrase *At the shockingly young age* in the subsequent paragraph that this information is intended to introduce the reader to what Joseph Pulitzer had been doing previously. The prediction is centered on Pulitzer, not *conflicts* or *contemporary journalism,* so eliminate (C) and (D). Choice (A) is a trap answer, for while it uses Pulitzer's name, the lines in question do not explain his *change in career.* Choice (B) is the correct answer.

38. **D** The question asks what specific details lines 41–44 reveal about Pulitzer, so read the reference window to make a prediction. The prediction will refer to his *shockingly young age.* Only *precociousness* matches this prediction, so eliminate (A), (B), and (C). Choice (D) is the correct answer.

39. **C** The question asks what the specific *misfortune* is in lines 64–69, so read the reference window to make a prediction. According to the passage, the *battle soured him on this kind of sensationalist journalism,* so the prediction should show that the misfortune was uncharacteristic in terms of

Pulitzer's overall career. There is no reference to Pulitzer having *lost the circulation battle*, so eliminate (A). Choice (B) is the opposite of the prediction, so eliminate it. The *misfortune* was Pulitzer's, not *many journalists*'; eliminate (D). Choice (C) is the correct answer.

40. **B** The question asks for a description of the comment in lines 93–95, so read the reference window to make a prediction. The prediction can be determined by the word *disappointed,* which shows that there is a criticism. There is only a statement, not an *overstatement* or a *hypothesis*; eliminate (A) and (C). The author also is not conceding anything, so eliminate (D). Choice (B) is the correct answer.

41. **C** The question asks what *the hope* refers to, so this is a context question. Context questions ask why an author used a specific word or phrase. The prediction will match the author's desire to *restore journalism to its rightful place as teller of things.* There is no reference to *corporate interests* or *societal change,* so eliminate (A) and (D). The author speaks about journalism and reporting as an industry, not just *a brave individual*; eliminate (B). Choice (C) is the correct answer.

42. **D** Note that the following question is a best evidence question, so this question and Q43 can be answered in tandem. This question asks what *the author (is) most likely to see as an unfortunate consequence of modern journalistic practices,* so the prediction must have to do with current affairs in journalism. Look at the answers for Q43 first. Choice (43B) is simply a biographical note about Pulitzer, so eliminate (43B). Choice (43C) also refers to a historical occurrence, not *modern journalistic practices;* eliminate (43C). *He would surely be disappointed* indicates that it is the perspective of Pulitzer, which is not possible, so eliminate (43D). The notion that *those who were previously tasked with dredging up the cold hard facts are now much more likely to provide viewers with predetermined opinions and personal perspectives* addresses a contemporary issue, so keep (43A). Return to Q42 and find an answer that matches the concern over *predetermined opinions.* There is no contrast between rural and urban, so eliminate (42A). In addition, no reference to *popularity* or *public scrutiny* is made; eliminate (42B) and (42C). If a journalistic entity *claims to be fair to all political* ideologies but *represents the viewpoints of only one political perspective,* its opinions are in fact predetermined. Choices (42D) and (43A) are the correct answers.

43. **A** (See explanation above)

Vocab Check

Here is a list of challenging words from Drill 4. If you don't know the definitions, look them up to learn them!

obstinate   decry   precociousness   critique   objectivity

Reading Practice Passage 1

Many articles and books have been written proposing a major revamping of the nation's school system. In this excerpt, the author presents his own views on this subject.

When nearly everybody agrees on something, it probably isn't so. Nearly everybody agrees: It's going to take a revolution to fix America's public
Line schools. From the great national think tanks to
5 the neighborhood PTA, the call to the barricades is being trumpeted. Louis V. Gerstner Jr., head of RJR Nabisco and one of the business leaders in education reform, proclaims the Noah Principle: "No more prizes for predicting rain. Prizes only
10 for building arks. We've got to change whole schools and the whole school system."

But it isn't so; most of that is just rhetoric. In the first place, nobody really wants a revolution. Revolution would mean junking the whole
15 present structure of education overnight and inventing a new one from scratch, in the giddy conviction that anything must be an improvement—no matter what it costs in terms of untaught kids, wrecked careers, and doomed
20 experiments. What these folks really want isn't revolution but major reform, changing the system radically but in an orderly fashion. The changes are supposed to be tested in large-scale pilot programs—Gerstner's "arks"—and then installed
25 nationally.

But even that is just a distant gleam in the eye and a dubious proposition too. There's nothing like a consensus even on designing those arks, let alone where they are supposed to come to
30 ground. And anyone who has watched radical reforms in the real world has to be wary of them: Invariably, they take a long time and cost a great deal, and even so they fail more often than they succeed. In organizations as in organisms,
35 evolution works best a step at a time. The best and most natural changes come not in wholesale gulps, but in small bites.

What the think-big reformers fail to acknowledge is that schools all over the
40 country are changing all the time. From Head Start programs to after-school Big Brother/Big Sister projects to self-esteem workshops, it's precisely these small-scale innovations and demonstration programs that are doing the job,
45 in literally thousands of schools. Some of these efforts are only partly successful; some fail; some work small miracles. They focus varyingly on children, teachers, and parents, on methods of administration and techniques of teaching, on
50 efforts to motivate kids and to teach values and to mobilize community support. Some are relatively expensive; others cost almost nothing. But all of them can be done—and have been done.

The important thing is that local schools aren't
55 waiting for a revolution, or for gurus to decree the new model classroom from sea to shining sea. They are working out their own problems and making their own schools better. And anyone—teachers, parents, principals, school board
60 members—anyone who cares enough and works hard enough can do the same.

1

The primary purpose of the passage is to

A) present an alternative view of a widely-held belief.

B) refute the notion that change is needed.

C) describe several plans to implement an educational revolution.

D) uncover and analyze new flaws in an old system.

The quotation in lines 9–10 ("No more . . . arks") can best be interpreted to mean that Gerstner believes that

A) the present educational system is functioning adequately.

B) the focus should shift from describing problems to finding solutions.

C) trying to make predictions about what will happen is always counterproductive.

D) fixing the educational system requires financing new school buildings.

In line 12, "rhetoric" most nearly means

A) the art of persuasive speaking.

B) language that sounds good but has little content.

C) the use of figures of speech.

D) the tendency to question the truth.

The author uses the phrase "come to ground" (lines 29–30) to

A) extend an existing metaphor in order to complicate the way a situation has been portrayed.

B) point out how little common ground educational reformers and students share.

C) highlight the difficulty of establishing a timeline for school reform.

D) raise a question about where and how new schools will be built.

In line 36, "wholesale" most nearly means

A) cheap.

B) intended for institutions.

C) on a large scale.

D) unnatural.

Which best summarizes the idea of "small bites" (line 37)?

A) Changing the system radically but in an orderly fashion

B) Making the system gradually look more like it did in the past

C) Allowing children to choose from a variety of small classroom settings

D) Using modest innovations to improve schools

Which choice provides the best evidence for the answer to the previous question?

A) Lines 2–4 ("Nearly . . . schools")

B) Lines 20–22 ("What . . . fashion")

C) Lines 40–45 ("From . . . schools")

D) Lines 47–51 ("They . . . support")

The programs mentioned in lines 40–42 are examples of

A) small-scale programs that make it possible for graduates to earn jobs.

B) "arks" that Louis V. Gerstner Jr. would approve of.

C) after-school projects that are only partly successful.

D) ways that local schools are finding solutions to educational problems.

The last paragraph of the passage develops a contrast between

A) conventional classrooms and those that incorporate natural elements.

B) those who call for revolution and those who find small steps to fuel the evolution of education.

C) caring about education and working hard to get an education.

D) waiting for change and decreeing how it will be achieved.

The author of this passage would most likely agree with which of the following statements?

A) Success in business does not qualify someone to make educational policy.

B) Very few people are qualified to improve the educational system.

C) A comprehensive national curriculum is an important step in improving the educational system.

D) Examples of effective educational reform already exist.

Reading Practice Passage 2

Questions 11–20 are based on the following passage.

This passage describes the first detailed observations of the surface of the planet Mars—observations that indirectly led some to the mistaken belief that intelligent life existed there.

The summer of 1877 had been an exceptional time for observing Mars. Every 26 months the slower-moving Mars comes especially close to
Line
5 Earth, creating the most favorable opportunity for observations—or, in the space age, for travel to the planet. Sometimes these opportunities are better than others. Because of the large ellipticity* of the Martian orbit, the distance between Mars and Earth at the closest approach of opposition
10 (when Mars is on the opposite side of Earth from the Sun) varies from as near as 35 million miles to as far as 63 million. The closest of these oppositions occurs approximately every 15 years, and 1877 was one of those choice viewing times.
15 Among the astronomers taking advantage of the opportunity was Giovanni Virginio Schiaparelli, director of Milan's Brera Observatory and a scientist highly esteemed, particularly for his research concerning meteors
20 and comets. While examining Mars with a relatively small 8-inch telescope, Schiaparelli saw faint linear markings across the disc. Earlier observers had glimpsed some such streaks, but nothing as prominent and widespread as those
25 Schiaparelli described seeing. His drawings of Mars showed the dark areas, which some took to be seas, connected by an extensive network of long straight lines. Schiaparelli called the lines *canali*.
30 In Italian, the primary meaning of *canali* is "channels" or "grooves," which is presumably what Schiaparelli intended in the initial announcement of his discovery. He said that they "may be designated as *canali* although we
35 do not yet know what they are." But the word can also mean "canal," which is how it usually was translated. The difference in meanings had tremendous theoretical implications.

"The whole hypothesis was right there in the
40 translation," science writer Carl Sagan has said. "Somebody saw canals on Mars. Well, what does that mean? Well, canal—everybody knows what a canal is. How do you get a canal? Somebody builds it. Well, then there are *builders* of canals on
45 Mars."
It may be no coincidence that the Martian canals inspired extravagant speculation at a time when canal-building on Earth was a reigning symbol of the Age of Progress. The Suez Canal
50 was completed in 1869, and the first efforts to breach Central America at Nicaragua or Panama were being promoted. To cut through miles of land and join two seas, to mold imperfect nature to suit man—in the nineteenth-century way of
55 thinking, this was surely how intelligent beings met challenges, whether on Earth or on Mars.
Schiaparelli seemed to be of two minds about the markings. Of the canal-builders' interpretation he once remarked, "I am careful
60 not to combat this suggestion, which contains nothing impossible." But he would not encourage speculation. At another time, Schiaparelli elaborated on observations suggesting to him that the snows and ice of the Martian north pole
65 were associated with the canals. When snows are melting with the change of season, the breadth of the canals increases and temporary seas appear, he noted, and in the winter the canals diminish and some of the seas disappear. But he saw a
70 thoroughly natural explanation for the canals. "It is not necessary to suppose them to be the work of intelligent beings," he wrote in 1893, "and notwithstanding the almost geometrical appearance of all of their system, we are now
75 inclined to believe them to be produced by the evolution of the planet, just as on Earth we have the English Channel."
His cautionary words had little effect. Those who wanted to believe in a system of water canals
80 on Mars, built by intelligent beings, were not to be discouraged—or proven wrong—for another 70 years.
* Ellipticity refers to an oval (rather than a perfectly round) orbit around the sun.

Oppositions of Mars, 1995–2031

Date of Opposition	Closest Distance (Millions of Miles)	Date of Opposition	Closest Distance (Millions of Miles)
February 12, 1995	62.8	April 8, 2014	57.4
March 17, 1997	61.3	May 22, 2016	46.8
April 24, 1999	53.8	July 27, 2018	35.8
June 13, 2001	41.8	October 13, 2020	38.6
August 28, 2003	34.6	December 8, 2022	50.6
November 7, 2005	43.1	January 16, 2025	59.7
December 24, 2007	54.8	February 19, 2027	63.0
January 29, 2010	61.7	March 25, 2029	60.2
March 3, 2012	62.6	May 4, 2031	51.4

11

Which choice best describes the developmental pattern of the passage?

A) A long-held but erroneous belief is introduced and debunked.

B) The circumstances that led to an incorrect interpretation of reported data are presented.

C) An example of the consequences of jumping to conclusions too quickly is provided as a warning.

D) An astronomical phenomenon is detailed and its potential consequences are explored.

12

In line 14, "choice" most nearly means

A) designated.

B) optional.

C) excellent.

D) favorite.

13

The passage indicates that which of the following is the definition of "*canali*" that Schiaparelli most likely intended?

A) Extensive networks

B) Dark sea-like areas

C) Long canals

D) Channels or grooves

14

Which choice provides the best evidence for the answer to the previous question?

A) Lines 25–28 ("His drawings . . . lines")

B) Lines 30–33 ("In Italian . . . discovery")

C) Lines 35–37 ("But . . . translated")

D) Lines 41–43 ("Somebody . . . canal")

15

The author quotes Carl Sagan in lines 39–45 primarily to

A) introduce a modern writer's views into the discussion.

B) illustrate the thought process that led to a particular interpretation.

C) call into question Schiaparelli's observations.

D) indicate how difficult it is to translate scientific observations into another language.

Which statement best summarizes the point made in the fifth paragraph?

A) The sightings of the Mars canals in 1877 led to a surge of canal-building on Earth.

B) The Suez Canal's completion in 1869 set in motion another canal-building project that ultimately became the Panama Canal.

C) Canal-building in the nineteenth century was a feat of engineering with significant cultural implications.

D) The readiness to believe that the *canali* were constructed by intelligent beings may have come from a general fascination with canal-building at the time.

In line 57, "of two minds" is used to indicate that Schiaparelli was

A) skeptical.

B) tentative.

C) undecided.

D) changeable.

To what did Schiaparelli attribute the periodic changes in appearance of the Martian canals described in the sixth paragraph?

A) Melted ice from the north pole flowing into the canals during some seasons, enlarging them

B) The ellipticity of the Martian orbit exerting a tidal pull on the water in the canals

C) The visual distortion of Schiaparelli's relatively small telescope not allowing Schiaparelli to see the Martian surface clearly

D) Changes in the distance between Earth and Mars making objects appear larger or smaller

Based on the table and passage, which choice would the author consider a "choice viewing time" to see Mars from Earth?

A) August 28, 2003

B) December 24, 2007

C) March 3, 2012

D) February 19, 2027

Which statement from the passage is most directly reflected by data presented in the table?

A) Lines 1–2 ("The summer . . . Mars")

B) Lines 6–7 ("Sometimes . . . than others")

C) Lines 12–13 ("The closest . . . years")

D) Line 14 ("1877 . . . viewing times")

Reading Practice Passage 3

The following passage gives a critical overview of the work of Frank Lloyd Wright, one of America's most famous architects. It has been adapted from "Frank Lloyd Wright—Twenty Years After His Death," published in *The New York Times,* April 15, 1979.

It is 30 years since Frank Lloyd Wright died at 91, and it is no exaggeration to say that the United States has had no architect even roughly
Line comparable to him since. His extraordinary
5   72-year career spanned the shingled Hillside Home School in Wisconsin in 1887 to the Guggenheim Museum built in New York in 1959.

His great early work, the prairie houses of
10   the Midwest in which he developed his style of open, flowing spaces and great horizontal planes, and integrated structure of wood, stone, glass, and stucco, were mostly built before 1910. Philip Johnson once insulted Wright by calling him
15   "America's greatest nineteenth-century architect." But Mr. Johnson was then a partisan of the sleek, austere International Style that Wright abhorred. Now, the International Style is in disarray, and what is significant here is that Wright's reputation
20   has not suffered much at all in the current antimodernist upheaval.

One of the reasons that Wright's reputation has not suffered too severely in the current turmoil in architectural thinking is that he
25   spoke a tremendous amount of common sense. He was full of ideas that seemed daring, almost absurd, but which now in retrospect were clearly right. Back in the 1920s, for example, he alone among architects
30   and planners perceived the great effect the automobile would have on the American landscape. He foresaw "the great highway becoming, and rapidly, the horizontal line of a new freedom extending from ocean to ocean,"
35   as he wrote in his autobiography of 1932. Wright wrote approvingly of the trend toward decentralization, which hardly endears him to today's center-city-minded planners—but if

his calls toward suburban planning had been
40   realized, the chaotic sprawl of the American landscape might today have some rational order to it.

Wright was obsessed with the problem of the affordable house for the middle-class
45   American. It may be that no other prominent architect has ever designed as many prototypes of inexpensive houses that could be mass-produced; unlike most current high stylists, who ignore the boredom of suburban tract
50   houses and design expensive custom residences in the hope of establishing a distance between themselves and mass culture, Wright tried hard to close the gap between the architectural profession and the general public.

55   In his modest houses or his grand ones, Wright emphasized appropriate materials, which might well be considered to prefigure both the growing preoccupation today with energy-saving design and the surge of interest
60   in regional architecture. Wright, unlike the architects of the International Style, would not build the same house in Massachusetts that he would build in California; he was concerned about local traditions, regional climates, and
65   so forth. It is perhaps no accident that at Taliesin, Wright's Scottsdale, Ariz., home and studio, which continues to function, many of the younger architects have begun doing solar designs, a logical step from Wright's work.

21

The main purpose of the passage is to

A) argue that Frank Lloyd Wright has never received sufficient appreciation.

B) draw attention to a little known but remarkable American architect.

C) assess a prolific career some years after its end.

D) highlight the errors made by Frank Lloyd Wright's detractors.

In the passage, the author anticipates which of the following objections to a point made in the passage about Wright's career?

A) The consequences of decentralization were not entirely positive.

B) Prairie houses are not appropriate for many regions of America.

C) Homebuyers are uncomfortable with the idea of inexpensive, mass-produced housing.

D) The gap between the architectural profession and mass culture cannot and perhaps should not be closed.

Which choice provides the best evidence for the answer to the previous question?

A) Lines 9–13 ("His great . . . 1910")

B) Lines 13–17 ("Philip . . . abhorred")

C) Lines 36–38 ("Wright . . . planners")

D) Lines 43–48 ("Wright . . . mass-produced")

24

Philip Johnson's quotation about Wright (line 15) was an insult because

A) Johnson felt Wright was responsible for much of the disarray of the antimodernist upheaval.

B) Johnson's remark implies that Wright's contributions to twentieth-century architecture were not as noteworthy as his earlier contributions.

C) urban and suburban space constraints rendered the open, flowing space of prairie houses obsolete in the twentieth century.

D) Johnson did not believe the automobile would have a positive effect on American architecture.

As used in line 16, "partisan" most nearly means

A) modernist.

B) critic.

C) weapon.

D) proponent.

The main purpose of the third paragraph (lines 22–42) is to

A) assess Wright's role in the early development of suburban planning.

B) assert and illustrate a claim about why Wright's reputation has not greatly declined.

C) bemoan the mistakes made by those who did not heed Wright's warnings.

D) contextualize some of Wright's more outdated ideas about architecture.

The author includes the reference to "high stylists" (line 48) primarily in order to

A) contrast Wright's practices with those of contemporary architects of comparable theoretical conviction.

B) decry the practices of some of the architects who have worked since Wright's death.

C) show the extent to which many other architects share Wright's obsession with affordable middle-class American housing.

D) distinguish between architects who design original structures and those who remodel existing buildings.

It can be inferred that the architects of the International Style would

A) resent the way Wright's reputation has not suffered to the extent their reputations have.

B) never use mass-produced or inexpensive materials.

C) regret the extent to which architecture has become less sleek and more focused on an aesthetics of messiness.

D) regard style as determined by factors other than the particulars of a proposed building site.

Which choice provides the best evidence for the answer to the previous question?

A) Lines 1–4 ("It is . . . since")

B) Lines 18–21 ("Now . . . upheaval")

C) Lines 47–54 ("inexpensive . . . public")

D) Lines 60–65 ("Wright . . . forth")

It can be inferred from the passage that "appropriate materials" (line 56) are materials that

A) can be mass-produced.

B) are suitable based on a site's climate, history, and resources.

C) incorporate resource-conserving features such as solar panels and xeriscape design.

D) reflect the prairie and desert landscapes that inspired Wright's greatest work.

Reading Practice Passage 4

In the following adapted excerpt from Anne Tyler's "Dinner at the Homesick Restaurant," Pearl, an elderly woman, is speaking to her son.

Pearl opened her eyes when Ezra turned a page of his magazine. "Ezra," she said. She felt him grow still. He had this habit—he had always

Line had it—of becoming totally motionless when
5 people spoke to him. It was endearing but also in some ways a strain, for then whatever she said to him ("I feel a draft," or "the paper boy is late again") was bound to disappoint him, wasn't it? How could she live up to Ezra's expectations? She
10 plucked at her quilt. "If I could just have some water," she told him.

He poured it from the pitcher on the bureau. She heard no ice cubes clinking; they must have melted. Yet it seemed just minutes ago that he'd
15 brought in a whole new supply. He raised her head, rested it on his shoulder, and tipped the glass to her lips. Yes, lukewarm—not that she minded. She drank gratefully, keeping her eyes closed. His shoulder felt steady and comforting.
20 He laid her back down on the pillow.

"Dr. Vincent's coming at ten," he told her.

"What time is it now?"

"Eight-thirty."

"Eight-thirty in the morning?"
25 "Yes."

"Have you been here all night?" she asked.

"I slept a little."

"Sleep now. I won't be needing you."

"Well, maybe after the doctor comes."
30 It was important to Pearl that she deceive the doctor. She didn't want to go to the hospital. Her illness was pneumonia, she was almost certain; she guessed it from a past experience. She recognized the way it settled into her back. If
35 Dr. Vincent found out he would take her out of her own bed, her own house, and send her off to Union Memorial, tent her over with plastic. "Maybe you should cancel the doctor altogether," she told Ezra. "I'm very much improved, I
40 believe."

"Let him decide that."

"Well, I know how my own self feels, Ezra."

"We won't argue about it just now," he said.

He could surprise you, Ezra could. He'd let a
45 person walk all over him but then display, at odd moments, a deep and rock-hard stubbornness. She sighed and smoothed her quilt. Wasn't it supposed to be the daughter who came and nursed you? She knew she should send him away
50 but she couldn't make herself do it. "I guess you want to get back to that restaurant," she told him.

"No, no."

"You're like a mother hen about that place," she said. She sniffed. Then she said, "Ezra, do
55 you smell smoke?"

"Why do you ask?" he said (cautious as ever).

"I dreamed the house burned down."

"It didn't really."

"Ah."
60 She waited, holding herself in. Her muscles were so tense, she ached all over. Finally she said, "Ezra?"

"Yes, Mother?"

"Maybe you could just check."
65 "Check what?"

"The house, of course. Check if it's on fire."

31

Which choice best summarizes the passage?

A) A woman makes stilted conversation with her son, all the while wishing her daughter could be with her.

B) A mother and son make small talk while pretending they are not concerned about a rash of arson attempts in the neighborhood.

C) A mother asks her son questions to try to discover the extent to which he is deceiving her.

D) A woman awakens and talks to her son while she is preoccupied by concerns that she does not express directly to him.

32

Pearl's attitude toward Ezra can best be described as

A) covert hostility.

B) condescension concealed by passivity.

C) apathetic resignation.

D) affection mixed with discomfort.

33

The action described in the passage takes place

A) in the apartment above the restaurant Ezra owns.

B) in a nursing home.

C) in Pearl's house.

D) in a rural hospital of limited means.

34

As used in line 6, "strain" is closest in meaning to

A) great pull.

B) source of tension.

C) injury caused by overexertion.

D) kind.

35

In the second paragraph, the issue of ice cubes is important to Pearl primarily because

A) she is grateful they have melted to produce water she can drink.

B) she dislikes cold water.

C) their absence makes her aware that time has passed.

D) they give her an excuse to ask Ezra for his help.

36

It can be inferred from the passage that it is "important to Pearl that she deceive the doctor" (lines 30–31) because

A) she is reluctant to go on the camping trip her family has planned.

B) she is feeling much better after her sleep.

C) previous experience with pneumonia has taught her to distrust doctors.

D) she does not want to be put in the hospital.

37

Which choice provides the best evidence for the answer to the previous question?

A) Lines 21–29 ("Dr. Vincent's . . . comes")

B) Lines 31–37 ("She . . . plastic")

C) Lines 38–40 ("Maybe . . . believe")

D) Lines 41–46 ("Let . . . stubbornness")

38

The statement, "He could surprise you, Ezra could" (line 44) serves primarily to

A) highlight Pearl's sense that she knows Ezra very well and yet does not fully understand him.

B) draw attention to the narrator's lack of omniscience.

C) reinforce the characterization of Ezra as volatile.

D) show that Pearl has never really understood her son at all.

39

The references to the quilt in lines 10 and 47 primarily serve to

A) highlight the waning of Pearl's strength during her illness.

B) suggest her mental unrest is echoed by her movements.

C) inject physical activity to offset the slow nature of the conversation that makes up so much of the passage.

D) suggest Pearl is dissatisfied with the bedding now that she cannot do her own laundry.

The parenthetical observation "cautious as ever" in line 56 functions in the context of the passage to

A) reflect the way Pearl perceives Ezra as she interacts with him.

B) hint at Ezra's guilt about the fire he'd set the previous night.

C) reveal the extent to which Ezra is worried that his mother is losing her grip on reality.

D) reinforce that Pearl's fears about fire are justifiable.

READING PRACTICE: ANSWERS AND EXPLANATIONS

Reading Practice Passage 1

1. **A** Answer this question after work on the specific questions has provided a sense of the passage overall. The passage begins by observing that when *nearly everybody agrees on something, it probably isn't so*, which sets up the passage's main purpose of exposing the fallacies of what *everybody agrees* about regarding America's public schools. The passage does not refute the idea that *change* is needed—it refutes the idea that *revolution* is needed—so eliminate (B). The main idea relates to the fact that there is more than one way to envision and affect change in the school system, but the focus is not on describing several implementation plans, so eliminate (C). Since the passage is focused on existing ways to address problems, (D) can be eliminated. Choice (A) matches the prediction and is the correct answer.

2. **B** In the context of the Noah story, *predicting rain* would be predicting that something bad was coming, while *building arks* would be taking action to respond to the situation. In the context of Gerstner's entire comment, then, building *arks* must mean something like *change whole schools and change the whole school system*. Eliminate (A), since this is the opposite of what Gerstner believes. Eliminate (C), since Gerstner is commenting in particular on the situation regarding education and there's no evidence he thinks that making predictions is *always* counterproductive. Eliminate (D), which is too literal a reading of *building arks*, since there's no evidence that changing whole schools and the whole school system requires new school buildings to be built. Choice (B) matches the prediction and is the correct answer.

3. **B** The word *rhetoric* is used in a sentence that is dismissing Gerstner's claims as untrue, so in context, *rhetoric* must mean something like *things that aren't true*. While (A) and (C) do offer actual definitions of *rhetoric*, those definitions do not fit the context, so they can be eliminated. Choice (D) raises the question of truthfulness, but it is the author who is questioning the validity of Gerstner's claims, whereas when *rhetoric* is used in the sentence, the word is describing Gerstner's claims themselves. Choice (B) does touch on the idea that the content of Gerstner's claim is questionable, and as Gerstner is articulating what *almost everybody believes*, the ideas must be persuasive even if incorrect. The correct answer is (B).

4. **A** Question 2 asked about Gerstner's articulation of what the author calls *the Noah Principle*. Gerstner's description uses the ideas of *predicting rain* and *building arks* to describe his assessment of how problems in the educational system must be addressed; the passage's author continues to use the metaphor in the second and third paragraphs' discussion of the problems with Gerstner's claims. Eliminate (B), since there's no evidence on how the backgrounds of educational reformers and students compare. Eliminate (D), which interprets *ground* too literally. Since the extension of

Gerstner's metaphor is used in two paragraphs that elaborate on why what Gerstner said *isn't so*, (C) identifies a challenge that proponents of revolution face, but does not get at the main reason for extending the metaphor as (A) does. Eliminate (C); the correct answer is (A).

5. **C** The word *wholesale* appears in the assertion that the *best and most natural changes come not in wholesale gulps, but in small bites*. The opposition between *wholesale gulps* and *small bites* suggests that *wholesale* must mean either *not small* or *large*. Eliminate (A) and (B), which play on uses of *wholesale* that are not relevant in this context. Eliminate (D), which uses language from the sentence but does not reflect the sense of the word suggested by context. Choice (C) matches the prediction well and is the correct answer.

6. **D** The sentence containing the mention of *small bites* is preceded by and further develops the assertion that *In organizations as in organisms, evolution works best a step at a time*. It may be clear from this context that in terms of the overall passage, *wholesale gulps* must refer to the revolution that some reformers are demanding and *small bites* must be the smaller-scale attempts to solve educational issues. Because the options in question 7 are found throughout the passage, these two questions can be worked as a set of general paired questions. Choice (7A) notes that a lot of people think the school system needs revolutionary change, which has some connection to (6A). Choice (7B) contradicts (6A) and does not support any other answers in (6), so (7B) can be eliminated. Choice (7C) provides examples of *small-scale innovations* that are *doing the job* and thus supports (6D). Choice (7D) does not support any of the choices in (6) and can be eliminated. Since the support that (7A) provides for (6A) addresses only the *radical* aspect but not the *orderly* aspect of the change, (7A) and (6A) are weaker answers and they also describe the side of the revolutionaries, not the side of those taking small steps: both can be eliminated. The correct answer for question 6 is (D), and the correct answer for question 7 is (C).

7. **C** See the explanation for question 6.

8. **D** The sentence in which the examples are given provides the explanation that *these small-scale innovations and demonstration programs* are *doing the job*. Context reveals that *the job* must be changing the public school systems and these programs are doing that job in small ways that nevertheless work toward solutions. Eliminate (A), as the first part of the answer looks good, but there's no evidence that these programs help graduates earn jobs. Eliminate (B), since Gerstner's "arks" are the opposite of the kinds of programs mentioned in the examples. Eliminate (C), as the emphasis is on the small-scale nature of the programs, rather than the fact that not all are successful. Choice (D) matches the prediction and is the correct answer.

9. **B** The overall passage is contrasting the popular wisdom that problems with the educational system require revolutionary solutions to the actual experience of people who are attempting to address problems through small-scale and local fixes. The final paragraph sums up this idea, noting that *The important thing* is that local schools are doing what they can rather than waiting for large-scale revolution. Eliminate (A), as the idea of natural elements in classrooms is not addressed in the

paragraph or passage. Eliminate (C), as the contrasting groups in the passage both care about education; additionally, the passage discusses the education system, not the work that students do to get an education. Eliminate (D), for while those calling for revolution might be portrayed as making decrees, the other side is *not* waiting for change. Choice (B) best matches the prediction and is the correct answer.

10. **D** After answering the other specific questions, question 10 should be relatively straightforward to answer. The author of the passage is most likely to agree with a point that he or she makes in the passage, so check the answer choices to see which statement best matches what the passage actually says. Eliminate (A), (B), and (C), as there is no evidence in the passage to support these claims. Choice (D) makes a claim that the author has already made and is thus the correct answer.

Reading Practice Passage 2

11. **B** Answer this question after work on the specific questions has provided a sense of the passage overall. The passage is informative in tone and describes the circumstances of Schiaparelli's observations and how they came to be interpreted. Eliminate (C), which is too broad; there's no evidence that the author is primarily interested in making an example of the circumstances described. Eliminate (D), since the passage focuses on the process of interpreting astronomical observations, not on the consequences of the phenomenon itself. While the passage does discuss the origins of a *long-held but erroneous belief*, the author is more interested in discussing how the interpretation arose than in debunking it, so eliminate (A). Choice (B) matches the prediction and is the correct answer.

12. **C** The phrase *choice viewing times* describes the best opportunities to observe Mars from Earth, so *choice* must mean something like *best* or *very good*. Eliminate (A), (B), and (D), which do not match this prediction. Choice (C) is the best match for the prediction and is the correct answer.

13. **D** The word *"canali"* appears first on lines 29 and 30. The first sentence of the third paragraph states that *the primary meaning of* canali *is "channels" or "grooves," which is presumably what Schiaparelli intended*. Eliminate (A), (B), and (C), which do not match the prediction. Choice (D) restates precisely what the passage says and is the correct answer.

14. **B** This question is the second in a specific paired set. In answering question 13, you should have underlined the exact place in the passage where you found the evidence to support your answer. That information is contained in lines 30–33, which matches (B). Eliminate (A), (C), and (D). Choice (B) is the correct answer.

15. **B** The quotation from Sagan makes up the bulk of the fourth paragraph. The third paragraph ends with the assertion that the *difference in meanings had tremendous theoretical implications*. Sagan's quote serves to illustrate how one translation—canals—led to *The whole hypothesis* about life on Mars. Since Sagan's comments don't refer to Schiaparelli's observations themselves, eliminate (C). Since the focus is on the implications of a particular translation rather than the difficulty of making such translations generally, eliminate (D). Sagan *is* a modern writer, but the *primary* purpose of

quoting his comments is to show the implications of the translation, not to provide modern commentary, so eliminate (A). Choice (B) best matches the prediction and is the correct answer.

16. **D** The fifth paragraph marks a shift from explaining the logic that led people from a translation of Schiaparelli's *canali* as canals to speculation about the makers of those canals. The first sentence of the fifth paragraph offers further context to explain why such logic may have taken hold: Schiaparelli's observations of Mars occurred *at a time when canal-building on Earth was a reigning symbol of the Age of Progress*. The examples that follow further develop this context. Eliminate (A), as it is the canal-building that may have led to the interest in the canals on Mars, rather than the reverse. Eliminate (B), as there is no evidence that the building of one canal caused the building of the other, and the relationship between the two canals is not the main idea of the paragraph. Eliminate (C), which is a statement that may be true, but which is not the main point of the paragraph. Choice (D) matches the prediction and is the correct answer.

17. **C** The referenced sentence notes that *Schiaparelli seemed to be of two minds about the markings*. The sentences that follow note that he was *careful* not to deny the validity of the canal-builders theory but would not encourage such speculation. Since he was reluctant to endorse the canal-building theory and could envision other causes of the observed phenomenon but yet would not speak against the canal-building theory, *of two minds* must means something like *unwilling or unable to commit to a side*. The answer that most closely matches this prediction is (C), *undecided*. Choice (D) can be eliminated because there's no evidence that he changed his mind, but rather that he did not decide at all. Though Schiaparelli might have been *skeptical* of one side of the debate, *of two minds* suggests that he did not choose a side, and says little of the manner in which he approached the debate; eliminate (A). Similarly, while Schiaparelli might have been *tentative* in approaching the hypotheses, the phrase *of two minds* is linked by evidence to the fact that he did not endorse either, so eliminate (B). Choice (C) matches the prediction and is the correct answer.

18. **A** The previous question focused on the fact that Schiaparelli did not choose a side in the debate about the origin of the canals on Mars, as described at the start of the sixth paragraph. Looking immediately after where that answer was found shows that the author also states that at another time, Schiaparelli noted that the changes in the canals were consistent with what might be the melting of snow and ice at the Martian north pole during changes of seasons. This prediction matches well with (A), so keep it. The sixth paragraph does not mention the ellipticity of the Martian orbit (which is discussed in the first paragraph, so eliminate (B). There's no evidence that the size of Schiaparelli's telescope produced poor quality observations, so eliminate (C). There's also no evidence that Schiaparelli thought the distance between Earth and Mars affected his perception of the canals, so eliminate (D). The correct answer is (A).

19. **A** This question asks which of the dates the author would consider a *choice viewing time*. Use the lead words to find the window in the text and read carefully. The passage says that a *choice viewing time* is when Mars is closest to Earth. Use the table to determine which answer choice has the smallest distance between the two planets. Choice (A) is the only answer with a distance less than 40. The correct answer is (A).

20.   **C**   This question asks which statement is reflected by the data in the table. Go through each answer choice and eliminate any that aren't supported by the table. Choice (A) can be eliminated because 1877 is not on the table. Choice (B) could be true, but it isn't directly reflected by the data. Eliminate it. Choice (C) is directly supported, so keep it. Choice (D) can be eliminated for the same reason (A) was eliminated. The correct answer is (C).

Reading Practice Passage 3

21.   **C**   The blurb states that the passage is a *critical overview* of Wright's work, and the passage opens with the claim that *the United States has had no architect even roughly comparable to him* since his death 30 years before the passage's publication. The rest of the passage offers support for that claim by pointing out remarkable things about Wright's career. Eliminate (D), since the passage focuses on Wright's career, not on the arguments of his detractors. Eliminate (A) and (B), as there is no evidence in the passage that Wright *never* received sufficient appreciation or that he was *little known* during his career or after his death. Choice (C) matches the prediction well and is the correct answer.

22.   **A**   This is a general question followed by a "best evidence" question, so questions 22 and 23 can be answered together as a set of general paired questions. Question 22 asks for an objection the author thinks might be raised about Wright's career—that's a tricky question that becomes much easier when the questions are worked together. Choice (23A) does not raise any of the objections mentioned in the choices for question 22, so eliminate (23A). Choice (23B) contains Johnson's insult (and it would be a stretch to call this an objection), but the lines do not support any of the objections in the answers for question 22, so eliminate (23B). Choice (23C) refers to *decentralization*, noting both Wright's approval of the trend and that this approval *hardly endears him to today's center-city-minded planners*, so (23C) seems to support (22A). Choice (23D) contains phrases that appear in (22C), but neither the cited lines nor the passage as a whole addresses an objection based on the feelings of *homebuyers*. Eliminate (23D), and then eliminate (22B), (22C), and (22D), since none of those are supported by evidence from an answer choice in question 23. The correct answer for question 22 is (A), and the correct answer for question 23 is (C).

23.   **C**   See the explanation for question 22.

24.   **B**   Johnson insulted Wright by calling him *America's greatest nineteenth-century architect,* a remark that might sound a lot like a compliment. The most likely way for the words to function as an insult would be either that the term *architect* was insulting or that *nineteenth-century* was insulting. Since the passage also refers to Wright as an architect, the former seems unlikely, but the passage notes that Wright's career spanned from 1887 to 1959, so Johnson's comment could have been an insult if it was meant to signal that Wright's twentieth-century work was not also great. Eliminate (A) and (C), which both use words from the passage but make claims for which there is no evidence. Eliminate (D), since Johnson does not figure in the third paragraph, which is where the

discussion of the effects of the automobile occurs. Choice (B) matches the prediction well and is the correct answer.

25. **D** The word *partisan* is used in the sentence, *But Mr. Johnson was then a partisan of the sleek, austere International Style that Wright abhorred.* Since this statement follows the report of Johnson's remark about Wright and seems to be offered as context for the insult, it seems likely that, as Wright really disliked the International Style, Johnson probably liked it a lot. In context, *partisan* must mean something like *supporter* or *fan*. Eliminate (A), (B), and (C), since none of these match the prediction. Choice (D), *proponent*, has the sense of *advocate* or *someone who speaks on behalf of a theory or idea*, so it matches the prediction well and is the correct answer.

26. **B** The third paragraph begins with the assertion that one of the reasons Wright's reputation has not suffered too much is that *he spoke a tremendous amount of common sense.* The rest of the paragraph expands on that claim and then illustrates it with the example of Wright's ideas about the effects of cars on the American landscape. Eliminate (A), which is too specific; the purpose of the paragraph is to make and support a larger claim about Wright's reputation, not to focus on Wright's role in suburban planning. Eliminate (C), as the paragraph does not focus on *bemoaning* anything and the emphasis is not on the mistakes of others. Eliminate (D), as the paragraph highlights how many of Wright's ideas *in retrospect were clearly right*, not how they are *outdated*. Choice (B) matches the prediction well and is the correct answer.

27. **A** The words *high stylists* occur in the phrase, *unlike most current high stylists*, which signals that Wright is being compared to some current architects. Wright was a *prominent architect* who did focus on middle-class housing while, according to the passage, many current comparable architects *ignore the boredom of suburban tract houses.* Thus, the phrase *high stylists* is used to set up a comparison between Wright's work and the work of some current architects. Eliminate (B), since the purpose of referring to the other architects is highlighting an aspect of Wright's work, not *decrying* the practices of others. Eliminate (C), which contradicts the information in the passage. Eliminate (D), as there's no evidence that the *high stylists* are remodeling existing buildings. Choice (A) matches the prediction well and is the correct answer.

28. **D** This question asks what must be true based on what the passage says about architects of the International Style, so it could be treated as a lead word question. It is followed by a "best evidence" question whose answer choices are drawn from throughout the passage, though, so the two questions can be effectively answered by treating them as a set of general paired questions. Choice (29A) could be seen as a weak support for (28A), since the lines assert that no other architect has had a comparable career, but there's no support for the claim that any architects, of the International Style or otherwise, *resent* Wright, so eliminate (29A). Some of the language in and around (29B) is echoed in (28C), but (28C) depends on a too literal reading of the referenced lines. Eliminate (29B). The phrase *mass-produced* in (29C) might seem to connect to (28B), but the lines do not support the extreme statement in (28B) or the claims in any of the other answers, so eliminate (29C). Choice (29D) states that Wright was *concerned about local traditions, regional climates,* and other factors that meant he *would not build the same house in Massachusetts that he would build*

in California. Since this makes him *unlike the architects of the International Style,* those architects must have been willing to ignore or not pay attention to those factors. Thus (29D) supports (28D), since Wright's focus on regional architecture was not shared by the International Style architects. Eliminate (28A), (28B), and (28C), as none is well supported by evidence offered in the answers to question 29. The correct answer to question 28 is (D), and the correct answer to question 29 is (D).

29. **D** See the explanation for question 28.

30. **B** The passage connects Wright's emphasis on *appropriate materials* with contemporary concerns about *energy-saving design* and *regional architecture,* as well as *local traditions* and *regional climates.* In this context, *appropriate materials* must be materials that are local to an area and that reflect the area's history, tradition, and climate. Eliminate (A), as the reference to mass production does not occur in the relevant window. Keep (B), since it matches the prediction very well. Eliminate (C), as *resource-conserving* is only one aspect of what makes the materials appropriate, and (B) provides those aspects more fully. Eliminate (D), since *appropriate materials* would reflect the site in which a building were being constructed, rather than an area that was significant to Wright. Choice (B) matches the prediction well and is the correct answer.

Reading Practice Passage 4

31. **D** The overall passage details exchanges between a woman and her son as she wakes up after a night that he has spent sitting at her bedside. The passage provides many details of her thoughts during their exchanges but does not reveal details of the son's inner thoughts. Eliminate (A), as there is no evidence that Pearl wishes her daughter were present, only that she is thinking that the situation she finds herself in is one that usually involves a daughter taking on Ezra's responsibilities. Eliminate (B), since the fact that Pearl had a dream about the house being on fire does not support the idea that any arson attempts have occurred, let alone a number of them. Eliminate (C) because, while Ezra may surprise Pearl on occasion and while Pearl does wish to deceive the doctor, there is no evidence to suggest that Pearl thinks Ezra is deceiving her. Choice (D) matches the prediction well, as it reflects the fact that the narrator provides details of Pearl's preoccupations as well as the conversation between the pair; (D) is the correct answer.

32. **D** Pearl thinks that Ezra's habit of stilling himself when people speak to him is *endearing but also in some ways a strain,* and this tension between her love for him and the stress that his presence causes is reflected throughout the passage. Thus she also knows that *she should send him away* but cannot make herself do it, and she shows evidence of having observed him very closely and with affection, even though she does not fully understand him and cannot fully speak her mind to him. Eliminate (A), as there is no evidence that she is hostile toward her son. Eliminate (B), as her action when she sniffs in line 54 is not a reaction to him but rather a sign of her concern about fire after her dream; there's no evidence that Pearl looks down on Ezra. Eliminate (C), as there is no evidence that Pearl does not care about Ezra or that she has given up trying to influence her interactions with him. Choice (D) matches the prediction well and is the correct answer.

33. **C**   Lead words found in the answer choices—*hospital, house,* and *restaurant*—point to the paragraph from lines 30–40 as a likely source of evidence for this question. Within this paragraph, Pearl thinks that if Dr. Vincent *found out he would take her out of her own bed, her own house, and send her off to Union Memorial.* Since the evidence clearly indicates that she is in *her own bed* when the action takes place, eliminate (A), (B), and (D). Choice (C) matches the prediction and is the correct answer.

34. **B**   The word *strain* appears in Pearl's observation that Ezra's habit of stilling himself to listen is *endearing but also in some ways a strain.* This observation is followed by Pearl's recognition that the strain results from her sense that *whatever she said to him...was bound to disappoint him.* Thus, *strain* must mean something like *a cause of tension or discomfort.* Eliminate (A), (C), and (D), each of which provides a valid definition of *strain* but not a definition that is appropriate in this context. Choice (B) matches the prediction and is the correct answer.

35. **C**   The lead words *ice cubes* appear in the second paragraph, where it is noted that Pearl *heard no ice cubes clinking.* She realizes that they must have melted, even as she thinks that it seems like very little time has passed since Ezra brought fresh ice cubes in. When she drinks the water and finds that it is *lukewarm,* this confirms her theory that more time has passed than she'd thought—time enough for the ice cubes to melt and the water to become warmer. Eliminate (A), as there's no evidence that the ice cubes had to melt before Pearl had access to water and the emphasis in the paragraph is on her recognition that time has passed. Eliminate (B), since the fact that in this case Pearl does not mind that the water is lukewarm suggests that normally she might prefer cold water. Eliminate (D), as Pearl has already asked Ezra for a drink of water before she notices the absence of the ice cubes. Choice (C) matches the prediction well and is the correct answer.

36. **D**   This is a specific question that is followed by a "best evidence" question, so questions 36 and 37 can be worked as a set of specific paired questions. The sentence referenced in question 36 is the first sentence of a paragraph and is immediately followed by the statement *She didn't want to go to the hospital.* Pearl believes that she has pneumonia and thinks that *If Dr. Vincent found out he would take her out of her own bed, her own house, and send her off to Union Memorial.* Thus, Pearl wants to deceive Dr. Vincent to keep him from realizing that she has pneumonia, so that she can avoid going to the hospital. Eliminate (A), since the reference to *tent* in the paragraph refers to putting a cover over her hospital bed and not a tent intended for camping, so there is no support for (A) in the passage. Eliminate (B), as the evidence suggests that Pearl tells Ezra that she is feeling better in order to get him to cancel the doctor's arrival; if she were actually feeling better, she would not need to deceive the doctor. Eliminate (C) because while there is evidence that Pearl has had pneumonia before, there is no evidence that the result was a distrust of doctors. Choice (D) matches the prediction well and is the correct answer.

37. **D**   Since this is the second question in a set of specific paired questions, look for the answer choice that contains the evidence used to support the answer in question 36. Eliminate (A), (B), and (C). Choice (D) contains the lines that provide the evidence for why Pearl needs to deceive the doctor and is therefore the correct answer.

38. **A** Aside from the dialogue, most of the information presented in the passage reflects Pearl's thoughts and perspective, as no explanations are offered as to what Ezra is thinking or feeling during the passage. The referenced statement—*He could surprise you, Ezra could*—is followed by the observation that Ezra would *let a person walk all over him but then display, at odd moments, a deep and rock-hard stubbornness*. This suggests that Pearl has observed and thought about her son often, since it is clear here and elsewhere in the passage that she knows how he tends to behave, though she cannot always fully predict what he will do in a particular circumstance. Keep (A), as it matches the prediction. Eliminate (B), since the statement reveals more about Pearl's thinking than about the narrator's perspective. Eliminate (C), as there is no evidence in the passage that Ezra is *volatile*. Eliminate (D), which is too extreme: Ezra may surprise Pearl at times, but that does not mean she has *never understood her son at all*. The correct answer is (A).

39. **B** Both references to the quilt follow a moment in which Pearl is thinking about Ezra's personality. In the first, she *plucked* at the quilt after thinking about the strain that she sometimes feels in trying to live up to Ezra's expectations. In the second, she *smoothed* the quilt after thinking about the fact that sometimes Ezra can be surprisingly stubborn, as when he insists on the doctor's visit. In both instances, there's evidence that Pearl is feeling some unease in relation to her thoughts, which suggests that her interactions with the quilt reflect her inner restlessness or unease. Eliminate (A), as there's no evidence linking physical weakness to the actions with the quilt. Keep (B), as it matches the prediction well. Eliminate (C), as this answer does not match the prediction as well as (B) does and the actions with the quilt do not do much to insert physical activity into the scene. Eliminate (D), as there is no evidence that Pearl cannot do her own laundry or that she is dissatisfied with the bedding. The correct answer is (B).

40. **A** The phrase *cautious as ever* modifies the description of Ezra's manner of speaking to Pearl. Most of the narration in the passage reflects Pearl's thoughts and impressions about her current situation: all of Ezra's other actions are seen from Pearl's perspective, not his, so the observation here is also likely to reflect Pearl's perspective. Keep (A), because it matches the prediction. Choices (B) and (C) both suggest that the phrase might reveal Ezra's feelings, but there is no evidence in the passage to support the idea that Ezra is feeling *guilt* or that he is worried about his mother's *grip on reality*: eliminate (B) and (C). Similarly, the passage suggests that Pearl's fear of fire is based on a dream, not that it is a justifiable concern, so eliminate (D). Choice (A) is the correct answer.

Chapter 4
Reading
Practice Test

Reading Test

65 MINUTES, 52 QUESTIONS

Turn to Section 1 of your answer sheet to answer the questions in this section.

DIRECTIONS

Each passage or pair of passages below is followed by a number of questions. After reading each passage or pair, choose the best answer to each question based on what is stated or implied in the passage or passages and in any accompanying graphics (such as a table or graph).

Questions 1–10 are based on the following passage.

The following passage is an excerpt from a memoir written by writer John Burke, about the novelist Joseph Heller.

I became a fan of Joseph Heller's writing while I was a student in high school in the 1970s. His most famous book, *Catch-22*, was practically an anthem for
Line my friends and me. We had dissected it, sitting in the
5 park outside school, reciting certain key passages aloud and proclaiming to anyone who would listen that this was quite possibly the best book ever written. Nearly twenty years later I am not sure that we were wrong.

Heller created a modern-day anti-hero who was
10 a soldier trying to stay sane in the midst of a war in which he no longer believed. This spoke to my generation, growing up as we did during the turmoil of Vietnam, and—however you felt about the issue—his ideas were considered important.

15 I had spent many hours imagining what the man who had created the savage wit and brilliant imagery of that book would be like in person. I was soon to find out. To this day, I have no idea how it was arranged, but somehow an invitation to speak at my high school
20 was extended and duly accepted.

On the day, I made sure to be near the gate of the school to see him arrive. I was looking for a limousine, or perhaps an entourage of reporters surrounding the man whose dust-jacket picture I had scrutinized so
25 often. But suddenly, there he was, completely alone, walking hesitantly toward the school like just a normal person. He walked by me, and I was amazed to see that he was wearing rather tattered sneakers, down at the heel.

30 When he began speaking in the auditorium, I was dumbfounded, for he had a very heavy speech impediment.

"That can't be him," I whispered loudly to a friend. "He sounds like a dork."

35 My notions of a brilliant man at that time did not extend to a speech impediment—or any handicap whatsoever. Ordinary people were handicapped, but not men of brilliance. There was, in fact, a fair amount of whispering going on in the auditorium.

40 And then somehow, we began to listen to what he was saying. He was completely brilliant. He seemed to know just what we were thinking and articulated feelings that I had only barely known that I had. He spoke for forty minutes and held us all spellbound. I
45 would not have left my seat even if I could.

As I listened, I began to feel awaken in me the possibility of being more than I had supposed that I could be. With some difficulty I managed to get to the school gate again and waited for twenty minutes while
50 I suppose he signed autographs and fielded questions inside the auditorium. Eventually, he came out, as he had come in, alone.

I screwed up all my courage and called to him, "Mr. Heller."

55 He almost didn't stop but then he turned around and came over to me.

"I just wanted to say how much I enjoyed your book. "

CONTINUE ➤

He looked down at me in my wheelchair, smiled
60 as if it was the most normal thing in the world and
shook my hand. I think that day may have been very
important in the future direction of my life.

1

The main purpose of the passage is to

A) illustrate that authors do not make as much
   money as people may expect.

B) describe an event that may have changed the
   author's perception of himself.

C) prove that *Catch-22* is the best book ever written.

D) provide insight into the contrast between how
   people expect the famous to behave and how they
   actually do.

2

Which choice provides the best evidence for the
answer to the previous question?

A) Lines 4–7 ("We . . . written")

B) Lines 22–25 ("I was . . . often")

C) Lines 41–42 ("He was . . . . thinking")

D) Lines 61–62 ("I think . . . life")

3

Based on the information the passage provides about
Heller's novel, *Catch-22* can best be described as

A) a provocative book that appealed almost
   exclusively to young men.

B) a memoir whose appeal depended on readers'
   proximity to the events that had influenced its
   creation.

C) a novel whose brilliance might appeal to people
   who were not directly affected by U.S. involvement
   in Vietnam.

D) an inspiring and realistic account of one soldier's
   valor.

4

The author uses the phrase "however you felt about
the issue" (line 13) to signal

A) that not all critics agreed with the author's
   assessment of *Catch-22*'s excellence.

B) that the book was valued by the author and his
   friends because of its ability to stir up debate.

C) that the Vietnam War was the subject of much
   debate.

D) that books can generate strong emotional
   responses in readers.

5

The author quotes his own comment to his friend in
lines 33–34 primarily in order to

A) emphasize the strength of his initial reaction to
   Heller's speech.

B) suggest that the reason Heller almost didn't stop
   as he was leaving was that he had overheard this
   comment.

C) highlight the author's suspicion that Heller had
   sent a stand-in to deliver his speech.

D) inject some humor to counterbalance the overall
   somber nature of the passage.

6

The author describes Heller's speech (lines 30–45)
primarily in order to

A) show that the students' initial skepticism was
   overcome by their interest in what he was saying.

B) illustrate the powerful effect a good speaker can
   have.

C) provide a warning not to judge people by how
   they speak.

D) respond to charges that Heller's work is overrated.

7

Which choice provides the best evidence for the answer to the previous question?

A) Lines 30–32 ("When . . . impediment")

B) Lines 38–39 ("There . . . auditorium")

C) Lines 40–41 ("And then . . . brilliant")

D) Lines 43–44 ("He . . . spellbound")

8

In the context of the passage as a whole, it can be inferred that the most likely cause of the "difficulty" (line 48) the author had in returning to the school gate was the

A) effect of the emotions Heller's speech had generated.

B) crowd of other students who were waiting to see Heller's departure.

C) injury the author had sustained in the Vietnam War.

D) fact that he has limited physical mobility.

9

In line 50, "fielded" most nearly means

A) answered.

B) evaded.

C) asked.

D) caught.

10

It can be inferred from the passage that the most likely reason the author had to "screw up all [his] courage" (line 53) was that

A) he was embarrassed about his own speech impediment.

B) he greatly admired Heller.

C) he was afraid Heller would not respond to him.

D) he thought Heller would be annoyed to deal with another student.

CONTINUE

Questions 11–21 are based on the following passages.

The following two passages present two views of the funeral industry in the United States. The first passage is an excerpt from a book written in 1963 by a journalist and takes a hard look at funeral practices at the time. The second passage was written in the 1980s by a member of the funeral business and looks at the changes in the industry since the first book appeared.

Passage 1

Oh death, where is thy sting? O grave, where is thy victory? Where, indeed. Many a badly stung survivor faced with the aftermath of some relative's
Line funeral has ruefully concluded that the victory has
5 been won hands down by a funeral establishment—in disastrously unequal battle.

Much has been written of late about the affluent society in which we live, and much fun poked at some of the irrational "status symbols" set out like golden
10 snares to trap the unwary consumer at every turn. Until recently, little has been said about the most irrational and weirdest of the lot, lying in ambush for all of us at the end of the road—the modern American funeral.

If the dismal traders (as an eighteenth-century
15 English writer calls them) have traditionally been cast in a comic role in literature, a universally recognized symbol of humor from Shakespeare to Dickens to Evelyn Waugh, they have successfully turned the tables in recent years to perpetrate a huge, macabre, and
20 expensive practical joke on the American public. It is not consciously conceived of as a joke, of course; on the contrary, it is hedged with admirably contrived rationalizations.

Gradually, almost imperceptibly, over the years,
25 the funeral men have constructed their own grotesque cloud-cuckoo-land where the trappings of Gracious Living are transformed, as in a nightmare, into the trappings of Gracious Dying. The same familiar Madison Avenue language has seeped into the funeral
30 industry.

So that this too, too solid flesh might not melt, we are offered "solid copper—a quality casket which offers superb value to the client seeking long-lasting protection," or the "colonial Classic Beauty—18 gauge
35 lead-coated steel, seamless top, lap-jointed welded body construction." Some caskets are equipped with foam rubber, some with innerspring mattresses. One company actually offers "the revolutionary Perfect-Posture bed."

Passage 2

40 In the past 20 years, many of the questionable excesses of the funeral trade have been curbed: legislation and self-policing by funeral home associations have brought some measure of regulation to an industry that was at one time sadly deficient. And
45 yet, if the sharp practices of shoddy morticians are no longer cause for customers to "whirl in their urns," as Jessica Mitford once put it so trenchantly, I fear that we may have somehow tilted too far in the other direction.

True, the costs of funerals in the 1960s were
50 escalating out of all proportion to real value, but I am convinced that in our search for economy and avoidance of discomfort we have weakened a very important family rite. Consider the case of one funeral "park" in Southern California that has instituted
55 "drive-in" funerals. Believe it or not, you can view the remains, attend the chapel service, and witness the interment—all without leaving your car.

To the extent that measures such as these have cut costs, I would applaud, but in my opinion these
60 measures have also produced a disconnection from the real purposes of a funeral. The process of spending time mourning the dead fills a real need for the bereaved. There is a purpose to each of the steps of a funeral, and if there is a commensurate cost to those
65 steps, then so be it. These days it is possible to have a funeral without a service for friends and family to gather, without a graveside interment, even without a casket. More frequently now, families will ask that contributions to charity be made in lieu of flowers and
70 wreaths—without recognizing that buying flowers provides a chance for friends and relatives to show their concern in a more tangible way than a gift to charity.

Let us not forget that feelings are as important as
75 economy.

CONTINUE

11

The first paragraph suggests that the "sting" referred to in the question, "Oh death, where is thy sting?" (line 1) is

A) the suffering from which the dead are released.

B) the consequence of the bitterness when heirs fight over an inheritance.

C) the challenges and costs of dealing with the funeral industry.

D) the painful recognition of all that the dying leave behind.

12

It can be inferred from the passage that the "dismal traders" (line 14) are

A) undertakers.

B) shopkeepers.

C) famous writers.

D) practical jokers.

13

The phrase "Madison Avenue language" is used by the author of passage 1 (line 29) to describe language aimed at

A) distracting mourners from the pain of their losses.

B) persuading people to buy things they don't need.

C) evoking the nightmarish aftermath of sudden death.

D) helping people to live graciously even in their suffering.

14

The examples provided in the last paragraph of passage 1 primarily serve to

A) illustrate how many different casket options are available.

B) demonstrate that modern undertakers have a sense of humor.

C) point to some ironies in the way modern funeral trappings are marketed.

D) highlight the extent to which some caskets will delay the decaying of a corpse.

15

The primary purpose of the second passage is to

A) condemn some new practices as ineffective in terms of addressing the escalating costs of funerals.

B) speculate on how Jessica Mitford might respond to the recent changes in the funeral industry.

C) argue that recent cost-cutting measures have had a detrimental effect on how funerals serve the mourners.

D) suggest that the purposes of each step in a funeral be spelled out more clearly.

16

Which choice provides the best evidence for the answer to the previous question?

A) Lines 40–41 ("In the . . . curbed")

B) Lines 49–53 ("True . . . rite")

C) Lines 55–57 ("Believe . . . car")

D) Lines 68–70 ("More . . . wreaths")

17

In line 41, "curbed" most nearly means

A) brought under control.

B) made public.

C) eliminated.

D) allowed to proliferate.

CONTINUE

18

According to the second passage, the excesses of the funeral trade have been changed for the better as a result of the

A) passage of time.

B) institution of services such as drive-in funerals.

C) elimination of flowers and wreaths at services.

D) actions of legislators and trade associations.

19

The author of passage 2 cites the example of "drive-in funerals" (line 55) in order to

A) illustrate the kind of practices that are detrimental to an essential function of funerals.

B) condemn people who consent to mourn this way.

C) demonstrate the ways the funeral industry has changed for the better.

D) rebut claims that the funeral industry has failed to change in the past twenty years.

20

The phrase "in lieu of" (line 69) most nearly means

A) instead of.

B) as well as.

C) because of.

D) in the form of.

21

The authors of both passages are likely to agree that the funeral industry

A) preys on the suffering of the bereaved.

B) is unlikely to change.

C) engages in widespread shoddy practices.

D) was in a troubled state in the 1960s.

Questions 22–31 are based on the following passage.

Scientists, theologians, and lay persons have debated the origins of life on Earth for hundreds of years. The following passage presents one scientist's explanation.

How did the earliest, most primitive, forms of life begin? Let's start with the formation of Earth 4.5 billion years ago. We can allow the first few hundred
Line million years to pass while Earth settles down to more
5 or less its present state. It cools down and squeezes out an ocean and an atmosphere. The surrounding hydrogen is swept away by the solar wind, and the rain of meteors out of which Earth was formed dwindles and virtually ceases.
10 Then, perhaps 4,000 million years ago, Earth is reasonably quiet and the period of "chemical evolution" begins. The first live molecules are small ones made up of two to five atoms each—the simplest form of life we can imagine—a single-strand RNA
15 molecule.
Different scientific theories have been proposed as to how this molecule first came into being. In 1908 the Swedish chemist Svante August Arrhenius theorized that life on Earth began when spores (living, but
20 capable of very long periods of suspended animation) drifted across space for millions of years, perhaps until some landed on our planet and were brought back to active life by its gentle environment.
This is highly dramatic, but even if we imagine
25 that Earth was seeded from another world, which, long, long before, had been seeded from still another

world, we must still come back to some period when life began on some world through spontaneous generation—and we may as well assume that this
30 generation began on Earth.
Why not? Even if spontaneous generation does not (or, possibly, cannot) take place on Earth now, conditions on the primordial Earth were so different that what seems a firm rule now may not have been so
35 firm then.
What won't happen spontaneously may well happen if energy is supplied. In the primordial Earth, there were energy sources—volcanic heat, lightning, and most of all, sunshine. At that time, Earth's atmosphere
40 did not contain oxygen, or its derivative, ozone, and the Sun's energetic ultraviolet rays would reach Earth's surface undiluted.
In 1954 a chemistry student, Stanley Lloyd Miller, made a fascinating discovery that shed light on the
45 passage from a substance that is definitely unliving to one that is, in however simple a fashion, alive. He began with a mixture of water, ammonia, methane, and hydrogen (materials he believed to have been present on Earth at its beginning). He made sure his mixture
50 was sterile and had no life of any kind in it. He then circulated it past an electric discharge (to mimic the energy sources roiling the planet at that time). At the end of a week, he analyzed his solution and found that some of its small molecules had been built up to larger
55 ones. Among these larger molecules were glycine and alanine, the two simplest of the twenty amino acids. This was the first proof that organic material could have been formed from the inanimate substances that existed on Earth so long ago.

Amino Acids Found in Miller-Urey and Volcanic Spark Discharge Experiments

Amino Acid	Miller-Urey Experiment (1952)	Volcanic Spark Discharge (2008)	Proteinogenic? (able to build proteins)
Glycine	Yes	Yes	Yes
α-Alanine	Yes	Yes	Yes
β-Alanine	Yes	Yes	No
Aspartic Acid	Yes	Yes	Yes
α-Aminobutyric Acid	Yes	Yes	No
Serine	No	Yes	Yes
Isoserine	No	Yes	No
α-Aminoisobutyric Acid	No	Yes	No
β-Aminoisobutyric Acid	No	Yes	No
Valine	No	Yes	Yes
Isovaline	No	Yes	No

Note: The Volcanic Spark Discharge Experiment was done in 2008 by a student of Stanley Miller's. Miller's original vials, still sealed from the 1950s, were re-analyzed using the most recent techniques and technologies.

CONTINUE ➤

22

Which choice best reflects the overall sequence of events in the passage?

A) A theory is proposed, tested, and proved to be impossible; an alternative theory is then presented.

B) A difficult question is introduced and the reasons why the question is difficult to answer definitively are explored in some detail.

C) The assertion is made that a scientific conundrum is impossible to answer and several experiments are described as illustration of the futility of tackling the problem.

D) A challenging question is introduced, a theory is set forth, and its key limitation is raised before a second theory is put forward and a related experiment is described.

23

The author's assertion that "We can allow the first few hundred million years to pass" (lines 3–4) primarily reflects the author's sense that

A) humans have no way to fully measure or comprehend the long history of Earth.

B) it would take far too long to describe the history of Earth in detail.

C) the most relevant aspects of Earth's history for the purposes of the passage are those that emerged about 4 billion years ago.

D) time and tide wait for no man.

24

The author most likely views the theories of Svante August Arrhenius as

A) innovative and daring.

B) dramatic but too elaborate.

C) interesting but unlikely.

D) illogical and impossible.

25

The word "generation" in line 29 most nearly means

A) creation.

B) reproduction.

C) offspring.

D) forebears.

26

It can be inferred that the fact that in primordial times "Earth's atmosphere did not contain oxygen" (lines 39–40) is significant to the author's explanation primarily because

A) without oxygen, human life could not exist.

B) all energy sources produce more intense heat in the absence of oxygen.

C) the question of how oxygen made its way into Earth's atmosphere has not been answered definitively.

D) without oxygen, the atmosphere lacked ozone to block some of the Sun's rays.

27

The author uses the example of Stanley Lloyd Miller's experiment primarily to

A) introduce the idea that laboratory confirmation of a theoretical possibility exists.

B) suggest the need for further research in the field.

C) speculate about the materials that were present when the Earth was first created.

D) highlight the significance of amino acids in understanding the origins of life.

28

Which choice provides the best evidence for the answer to the previous question?

A) Lines 43–46 ("In 1954 . . . alive")

B) Lines 46–49 ("He . . . beginning")

C) Lines 52–55 ("At the . . .ones")

D) Lines 55–56 ("Among . . . acids")

29

The author's conclusion at the end of the last paragraph would be most directly supported by additional information concerning

A) what other chemical materials were present on Earth 4 billion years ago.

B) what factors might have kept life from emerging earlier.

C) whether other scientists were able to re-create Miller's experiments and achieve similar results.

D) whether the addition of other chemicals into Miller's initial mixture changed the experiment's outcome.

30

Which of the following claims is supported by the table?

A) More amino acids were discovered in the twentieth century than in the twenty-first century.

B) New technologies are able to detect more amino acids than were earlier technologies.

C) All the proteins discovered in the Miller-Urey experiment have the ability to form organic material.

D) The Volcanic Spark Discharge experiment found exactly twice as many amino acids as the Miller-Urey Experiment.

31

Information presented in the table most directly supports which idea from the passage?

A) Spores drifting across space landed on the planet and were brought back to life.

B) An energy source could prompt spontaneous generation of life from existing elements.

C) Because of the lack of oxygen in the atmosphere, the rays of early Earth's sun were undiluted.

D) The simplest lifeform imaginable is a single-strand RNA molecule.

CONTINUE

Questions 32–42 are based on the following passage.

The following passage relates some conclusions the author draws after listening to a seminar speaker denounce some modern conveniences for their negative effects on people's personal lives.

Several weeks ago, when the weather was still
fine, I decided to eat my lunch on the upper quad,
an expanse of lawn stretching across the north end
Line of campus and hedged in by ancient pine trees on
5   one side and university buildings on the other.
Depositing my brown paper lunch bag on the grass
beside me, I munched in silence, watching the trees
ripple in the wind and musing over the latest in a
series of "controversial" symposiums I had attended
10 that morning. The speaker, an antiquated professor
in suspenders and a mismatched cardigan, had
delivered an earnest diatribe against modern tools of
convenience like electronic mail and instant messaging
programs. I thought his speech was interesting, but
15 altogether too romantic.
     My solitude was broken by two girls, deep in
conversation, who approached from behind and sat
down on the grass about ten feet to my left. I stared
hard at my peanut butter sandwich, trying to not
20 eavesdrop, but their stream of chatter intrigued me.
They interrupted each other frequently, paused at
the same awkward moments, and responded to each
other's statements as if neither one heard what the
other said. Confused, I stole a glance at them out
25 of the corner of my eye. I could tell that they were
college students by their style of dress and the heavy
backpacks sinking into the grass beside them. Their
body language and proximity also indicated that they
were friends. Instead of talking to each other, however,
30 each one was having a separate dialogue on her cell
phone.
     As I considered this peculiar scene, this morning's
bleary-eyed lecturer again intruded into my thoughts.
His point in the symposium was that, aside from the
35 disastrous effects of emails and chatting on the spelling,
grammar, and punctuation of the English language,
these modern conveniences also considerably affect
our personal lives. Before the advent of electronic mail,
people wrote letters. Although writing out words by
40 hand posed an inconvenience, it also conferred certain

important advantages. The writer had time to think
about his message, about how he could best phrase it in
order to help his reader understand him, about how he
could convey his emotions without the use of dancing
45 and flashing smiley face icons. When he finished his
letter, he had created a permanent work of art to which
a hurriedly typed email or abbreviated chat room
conversation could never compare. The temporary,
impersonal nature of computers, Professor Spectacles
50 concluded, is gradually rendering our lives equally
temporary and impersonal.
     And what about cell phones? I thought. I have
attended classes where students, instead of turning off
their cell phones for the duration of the lecture, leave
55 the classroom to take calls without the slightest hint
of embarrassment. I have sat in movie theaters and
ground my teeth in frustration at the person behind
me who can't wait until the movie is over to give his
colleague a scene-by-scene replay. And then I watched
60 each girl next to me spend her lunch hour talking to
someone else instead of her friend. Like the rest of
the world, these two pay a significant price for the
benefits of convenience and the added safety of being
in constant contact with the world. When they have a
65 cell phone, they are never alone, but then again, *they
are never alone.*
     They may not recognize it, but those girls, like most
of us, could use a moment of solitude. Cell phones
make it so easy to reach out and touch someone
70 that they have us confused into thinking that being
alone is the same thing as being lonely. It's all right
to disconnect from the world every once in a while;
in fact, I feel certain that our sanity and identity as
humans necessitate it. And I'm starting to think that
75 maybe the Whimsical Professor ranting about his
"technological opiates" is not so romantic after all.

CONTINUE

32

The structure of the passage overall can best be characterized as

A) a narrative that traces the development of the author's ideas on a topic that is raised by some people the author encounters during the events described.

B) a balanced assessment of a theory that is introduced, considered, and ultimately debunked.

C) a short anecdote followed by the introduction of a theory and the presentation of evidence related to that theory.

D) a consideration of several sides of an issue that is generally understood to be outdated, followed by a conclusion that redefines the terms under discussion.

33

The author's ultimate attitude toward the symposium speaker can best be described as

A) assent tinged with irreverence.

B) puzzlement tinged by scorn.

C) disagreement coupled with dislike.

D) affection bolstered by nostalgia.

34

Which choice provides the best evidence for the answer to the previous question?

A) Lines 10–14 ("The speaker . . .programs")

B) Lines 32–33 ("As I . . . thoughts")

C) Lines 48–51 ("The temporary . . .impersonal")

D) Lines 74–76 ("And I'm . . . all")

35

In the context of the overall passage, the details about the setting in which the author sat to eat lunch serve primarily to

A) paint a picture in the reader's mind.

B) raise the question of whether the same conclusion would have been reached if the author had encountered the two girls in a busier, urban setting.

C) contribute to the author's growing awareness that there is some validity to what is initially portrayed as the speaker's antiquated or overly romantic viewpoint.

D) evoke a sense of an idyllic college campus.

36

The author's decision to use quotation marks around the word "controversial" in line 9 and to italicize the phrase "they are never alone" in lines 65–66 can best be described as

A) a variation in techniques that is intended to keep the reader's interest by avoiding too much repetition.

B) an inconsistency that might have been pointed out by a copyeditor.

C) a matter of personal preference that reinforces the author's whimsical approach to the material.

D) a desire to call the use of one term into question and to suggest an alternative interpretation of the other.

37

The main purpose of the third paragraph is to

A) link the symposium speaker's outdated argument to his age and fatigue.

B) contrast the modern attitudes of the girls on their phones with the antiquated ideas of the symposium speaker.

C) relate the events that occurred after the author encountered the two girls on their cell phones.

D) explain the main points of the symposium speaker's address.

CONTINUE ➡

38

Based on the information in the passage, with which of the following statements about the "dancing and flashing smiley face icons" mentioned in lines 44–45 is the symposium speaker most likely to agree?

A) The use of such icons in anything but the most informal message is inappropriate.

B) The use of such icons might result in less reflection and less attention to the finer points of language selection.

C) Such icons have no place in a work of art.

D) The tendency of such icons to both dance and flash illustrates the exaggerated nature of most computer-facilitated communication.

39

The author provides the instances listed in lines 52–61 primarily as examples of

A) pet peeves that the author believes many other people can relate to.

B) experiences in the author's life that offer support to the symposium speaker's thesis.

C) rude behavior that the previous generation would not have tolerated.

D) occasions that reveal the need for a new etiquette guide to be written for the digital age.

40

What is the "significant price" (line 62) that is paid by the two girls the author observes during lunch?

A) The relatively higher phone bills they pay for using so much data

B) The confusion caused by trying to carry on a phone conversation when surrounded by other people

C) The sacrifice of opportunities for introspection and solitude

D) The awkward pauses that sometimes emerge in phone conversations when one of the participants is distracted

41

Which of the following would be the best title for a speech countering the arguments of the "Whimsical Professor" (line 75)?

A) "The Romance of Written Communication"

B) "Ties That Bind: How Electronic Communication Brings Us Together"

C) "Spelling Reform for the Computer Age"

D) "Too Convenient?: Benefits and Costs of Instant Communication"

42

As used in lines 15 and 76, the word "romantic" most nearly means

A) concerned with expressions of affection and love.

B) having an academic interest in the Romantic period.

C) not directly or practically applicable to current circumstances.

D) not platonic.

CONTINUE

Questions 43–52 are based on the following passage.

Adapted from Bradley J. Phillips, Coronal Mass Ejections: New Research Directions. *Journal of Solar Research, 2009.*

The idea that the sun has an almost unambiguously benign effect on our planet appears, on the surface, to be an incontrovertible one. Few people realize,
Line however, that certain events on the sun can have
5 disastrous consequences for life here on Earth. The geomagnetic storm is one such phenomenon. These storms begin on the surface of the sun when a group of sunspots creates a burst of electromagnetic radiation. These bursts thrust billions of tons of ionized gas,
10 known as plasma, into space; scientists refer to these solar projections as coronal mass ejections (CMEs). After this initial explosion, the CME gets caught up in a shower of particles, also known as a "solar wind," that continuously rains down on the Earth from the sun.
15 The last recorded instance of a major CME occurred in 1989, when the resulting geomagnetic storm knocked out an entire electrical power grid, depriving over six million energy consumers of power for an extended period. As we become increasingly
20 dependent on new technologies to sustain ourselves in our day-to-day activities, the potential havoc wrought by a major CME becomes even more distressing. Scientists conjecture that a "perfect storm" would have the potential to knock out power grids across the globe
25 and create disruptions in the orbit of low-altitude communication satellites, rendering such satellites practically useless.

What troubles scientists most about these "perfect storms" is not only their potential for interstellar
30 mischief, but also the fact that they are so difficult to forecast. For one thing, remarkable though these solar occurrences might be, they are still a relatively rare phenomenon, and the few existing records regarding major CMEs provide researchers with scant
35 information from which to draw conclusions about their behavior. Solar storm watchers are frustrated by yet another limitation: time. CMEs have been known to travel through space at speeds approaching 5 million miles per hour, which means they can cover the 93
40 million miles between the sun and the Earth in well under 20 hours. (Some have been known to travel the same distance in as little as 14 hours.) The difficulties created by this narrow window of opportunity are compounded by the fact that scientists are able to
45 determine the orientation of a CME's magnetic field only about 30 minutes before it reaches the atmosphere, giving them little or no time to predict the storm's potential impact on the surface.

Some world governments hope to combat this
50 problem by placing a satellite in orbit around the sun to monitor activity on its surface, in the hopes that this will buy scientists more time to predict the occurrence and intensity of geomagnetic storms. In the meantime, many energy providers are responding to the CME
55 threat by installing voltage control equipment and limiting the volume of electricity generated by some power stations.

CONTINUE

Geomagnetic Storm Activity as Measured by Change in Disturbance Storm index (DST)

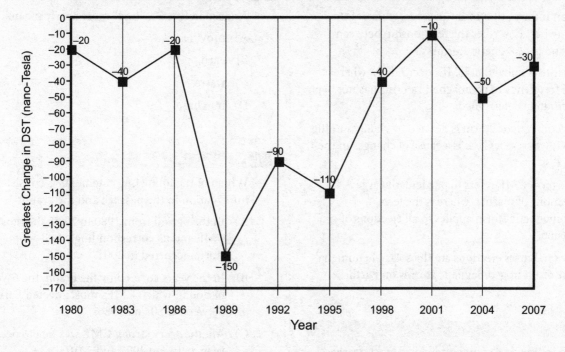

43

Over the course of the passage, the focus shifts from

A) detailing the more positive aspects of an astronomical phenomenon to enumerating the counterbalancing costs of the phenomenon.

B) describing a phenomenon in layman's terms to explaining the same phenomenon in scientific language.

C) introducing a relatively unknown danger to explaining the more challenging aspects of trying to address that danger.

D) warning of the dangers of a new phenomenon to celebrating the steps taken by governments to combat the dangers of that phenomenon.

44

The phrase "almost unambiguously benign" in lines 1–2 describes

A) the effect of the sun on the surface of Earth.

B) a failure to understand the effects of ultraviolet rays.

C) most people's understanding of the effects of the sun on Earth.

D) solar projections that are referred to as coronal mass ejections.

45

With which of the following statements would the author of the passage be most likely to agree?

A) If more people knew about the harm that CMEs might cause, governments would be better able to implement their plans to offset the dangers.

B) The negative effects of CMEs on humans are likely to continue to worsen.

C) Scientists will not be able to overcome the challenges created by the great speed at which CMEs travel.

D) The term *perfect storm* is fittingly ironic when applied to a storm that can cause such immense damage.

46

Which choice provides the best evidence for the answer to the previous question?

A) Lines 3–5 ("Few . . . Earth")

B) Lines 19–22 ("As we . . . distressing")

C) Lines 23–27 ("Scientists . . . useless")

D) Lines 37–41 ("CMEs . . . hours")

CONTINUE ➤

47

Based on information in the passage, which of the following best describes the relationship between CMEs and geomagnetic storms?

A) Scientists know that CMEs occur daily, whereas the frequency of geomagnetic storms has not been accurately determined.

B) A geomagnetic storm is defined by changes in the DST, whereas a CME is a cause of changes in the DST.

C) The term CME refers to particularly large ejections of plasma, whereas the term geomagnetic storm applies to all ejections of plasma.

D) Coronal mass ejections are the solar phenomena that result in geomagnetic storms on Earth.

48

As used in line 44, "compounded by" most nearly means

A) derived from.

B) undone by

C) combined with.

D) worsened by.

49

According to the passage, some governments seek to address the challenges of predicting when and how a CME will affect Earth by

A) developing a coordinating network of solar storm watchers to ensure that every CME is spotted as soon as it occurs.

B) moving as much as possible of the electrical power grid infrastructure underground.

C) placing a satellite in orbit around the sun.

D) installing voltage control equipment and increasing the volume of electricity generated by some power stations.

50

As used in line 52, "buy" most nearly means

A) provide.

B) earn.

C) waste.

D) purchase.

51

Which of the following statements is consistent with information in the passage and the graph?

A) In the period from 1980 to 2007, the most major CME and its correspondingly bad geomagnetic storm occurred in 2001.

B) In the years covered by the graph, the 6-year period in which CMEs most affected Earth was between 1980 and 1986.

C) Another very strong CME was due to occur in the years between 2007 and 2010.

D) The DST measure is inversely proportional to the strength of geomagnetic storm activity.

52

Which statement is best supported by the data presented in the graph?

A) One troubling aspect of CMEs is the difficulty in predicting when one will occur.

B) CMEs travel through space at speeds that approach 5 million miles per hour.

C) Only a storm as massive as the one that occurred at the end of the 1980s could wreak major havoc on the United States.

D) Scientists are currently able to determine the orientation of a CME's magnetic field less than an hour before the storm reaches Earth's atmosphere.

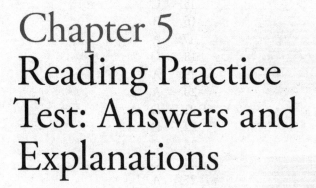

Chapter 5
Reading Practice
Test: Answers and
Explanations

READING PRACTICE TEST ANSWER KEY

1.	B	27.	A
2.	D	28.	A
3.	C	29.	C
4.	C	30.	B
5.	A	31.	B
6.	A	32.	A
7.	C	33.	A
8.	D	34.	D
9.	A	35.	C
10.	B	36.	D
11.	C	37.	D
12.	A	38.	B
13.	B	39.	B
14.	C	40.	C
15.	C	41.	B
16.	B	42.	C
17.	A	43.	C
18.	D	44.	C
19.	A	45.	B
20.	A	46.	B
21.	D	47.	D
22.	D	48.	D
23.	C	49.	C
24.	C	50.	A
25.	A	51.	D
26.	D	52.	A

EXPLANATIONS FOR THE READING PRACTICE TEST

1. **B** Question 1 is a general question and is followed by a "best evidence" question, so questions 1 and 2 should be worked together after the specific questions have been tackled. Choice (2A) could support (1C), but the passage overall focuses on the effect of Heller's visit, so the passage does not work to prove the author's estimation of the book. Eliminate (2A). Choice (2B) offers some support for (1D), but the lines do more to note a difference between expectations and reality than to provide *insight* into the contrast. Eliminate (2B). Choice (2C) describes the impression Heller made when he spoke to the students and does not support any of the choices in question 1. Eliminate (2C). Choice (2D) supports (1B), and both reflect the emphasis in the passage on the idea that Heller's visit had an impact on the author. Eliminate (1A), (1C), and (1D), as they are not supported by an answer choice in question 2. The correct answer for question 1 is (B), and the correct answer for question 2 is (D).

2. **D** See the explanation for question 1.

3. **C** This question is a little tricky; the key is to eliminate answers that contain details for which no evidence can be located. The description of *Catch-22* is primarily found in the first two paragraphs, so check the answer choices against the details found there. The author does note that the book was *practically an anthem* for his friend and him, but there is no evidence to support the more extreme claim that the book appealed *almost exclusively* to young men (or even that the author's friends were all male). Eliminate (A). The author does note that the book *spoke* to his generation, as they had grown *during the turmoil of Vietnam*, but there is no evidence that Heller's book is a *memoir*, nor does the author explicitly say that *Catch-22* was inspired by the Vietnam War. Eliminate (B). Heller's book features a *modern-day anti-hero* whose action during the book is described as *trying to stay sane in the midst of a war*; there is not additional evidence to show that this action is described realistically or that the main character demonstrates *valor*, so eliminate (D). While (C) might not seem like a strong answer, there is plenty of evidence that the author thinks Heller's novel is brilliant. His conviction 20 years later that his initial assessment of the book was not off base suggests that the book's appeal is not necessarily limited to those directly experiencing the effects of the war. Choice (C) is the correct answer.

4. **C** The indicated phrase is set off by dashes and, in the context of the sentence, functions as a further commentary on the topic that is mentioned right before the first dash, *the turmoil of Vietnam*. Eliminate (A) and (B), since the phrase is not making reference to the responses of critics or of the author and his friends to *Catch-22*. Eliminate (D) as too broad and also addressing reactions to books rather than reactions to the war. Choice (C) is the only answer that is consistent with the prediction that the indicated phrase comments on the nature of the Vietnam War. Choice (C) is the correct answer.

5. **A** The quoted lines come at the beginning of the account of Heller's speech and immediately follow the author's explanation that he was *dumbfounded* because Heller had *a very heavy speech impediment*. In the context of the description of the speech, the words serve to emphasize the strength

of the author's initial reaction by contrasting his admiration for Heller's book with his sense that Heller was *a dork*. Eliminate (B), as there's no evidence that Heller could overhear the author's comment. Eliminate (C), as there's no evidence in the passage to support the idea that the author's first sentence—*That can't be him*—should be taken literally. The author's comments might add humor as (D) suggests, but a stronger case can be made for (A), which matches the prediction. Eliminate (D). Choice (A) is the correct answer.

6. **A** This question is the first in a set of specific paired questions, so look in the indicated lines to answer question 6 first. Lines 30–45 describe the adverse initial reaction the author and others in the auditorium had when Heller began speaking. After describing that reaction and the reasons the author reacted as he did, the author describes how the audience's perception shifted: *And then somehow, we began to listen to what he was saying. He was completely brilliant.* The description of the occasion of the speech works to highlight this attitude. Eliminate (B) as too broad; the author is interested in the effect of Heller's speech, not in the effect of good speakers generally. Choice (C) is also too broad and there's no evidence elsewhere that the author is trying to *provide a warning*. Eliminate (C). Eliminate (D), as the author is discussing the reaction to Heller's speech, not his book. Choice (A) is consistent with the prediction and is the correct answer.

7. **C** This question is the second in a set of specific paired questions. The evidence for the answer to question 6 is found in lines 40–41. Choice (C) includes these lines. Eliminate (A), (B), and (D). The correct answer is (C).

8. **D** This question is tricky and might be easier if saved until questions 9 and 10 have been answered, as the process of answering those questions will provide a better sense of *the passage as a whole*. While the author says that he and the rest of the audience were *spellbound* during Heller's speech, there's no evidence that the author's response to the speech made it difficult to move to the gate. Eliminate (A). The author speculates that Heller was held up as he *signed autographs and fielded questions inside the auditorium*, but there's no evidence that others have come out to the gate. Eliminate (B). The author is still in high school when Heller comes to speak, and there's no evidence he served in Vietnam at any time. Eliminate (C). The author says of Heller's speech *I would not have left my seat even if I could*, and that statement coupled with the fact that he is in a wheelchair while he waits for Heller's exit supports the idea that the author was wheelchair-bound. Choice (D) is the correct answer.

9. **A** The word *fielded* appears in the phrase *signed autographs and fielded questions*. Since the author supposes this is what Heller did after his speech, *fielded* must mean something like *answered* or *responded to*. Choice (A) matches the prediction very well. Eliminate (B), (C), and (D) as there's no evidence that Heller did anything other than interact with his audience as speakers generally do after giving a speech. The correct answer is (A).

10. **B** To answer an inference question, look for the answer that must be true based on what the passage says. There's no evidence that the author had a speech impediment, only that Heller did. Eliminate (A). There's no evidence that the author was afraid that Heller wouldn't respond or that the author

anticipated that Heller would not want to deal with another student. Eliminate (C) and (D). There is ample evidence that the author greatly admired both Heller and his book, so (B) is most consistent with what the passage says and is the correct answer.

11.   **C**   The *sting* referred to in the opening question is echoed in the assertion later in the first paragraph that *Many a badly stung survivor faced with the aftermath of some relative's funeral has ruefully concluded* that the funeral industry has won the battle. Thus the author is identifying the *sting* of death as the unpleasant aspects of dealing with the funeral industry. Eliminate (A) and (D), as both refer to the experience of the dying, not the mourners of the dead. While (B) does explicitly mention *heirs*, it focuses on a struggle for inheritance among survivors, not a struggle with the funeral industry. Eliminate (B). Choice (C) matches the prediction and is the correct answer.

12.   **A**   This question is a bit tricky. The author does not spell out her meaning here, but the blurb notes that the passage is from a book that *takes a hard look at funeral practices* in the 60s. The second paragraph also ends with a reference to the *modern American funeral* and the fourth paragraph begins with a reference to the *funeral men*, so (A), *undertakers*, is most consistent with the structure and subject of the passage overall. The term *traders* could seem to connect with *shopkeepers*, but as *undertakers* also have goods and services to sell, (A) is stronger than (B), and (B) can be eliminated. While three famous authors are mentioned, their names are used as examples of writers who have *cast* the *dismal traders* in a *comic role in literature*. Eliminate (C). Similarly, while the passage says the dismal traders have perpetrated a practical joke, it also says that this joke is not *consciously conceived of as a joke*, so eliminate (D). The correct answer is (A).

13.   **B**   This question is also tricky, as it asks about one of the several allusions that the author makes in this passage. The reference to *Madison Avenue* may not trigger any associations, so check the passage to see what characteristics of *Madison Avenue language* are provided. The language is implicated in the creation of a *grotesque cloud-cuckoo-land* (whatever that is) that emphasizes the *trappings of Gracious Dying*. The fifth paragraph provides several illustrations of the kind of language the author is referring to, and the quotations are all examples of appealing language that describes things that are not really necessary. The dead do not need either *long-lasting protection* or elaborate mattresses, and particularly not mattresses intended to address posture issues. While this language might be *distracting* if mourners focused on it, there's no evidence that the language is intended to distract, so eliminate (A). There's no evidence that *sudden* death is of particular concern here, so eliminate (C). The language describes items that one uses only after death, not while dying, so eliminate (D). Choice (B) matches the prediction and is the correct answer.

14.   **C**   The work done to answer question 13 helps here. The illustrations in the last paragraph are all examples of items that sound appealing but that are not really necessary. The author signals at the end of the fifth paragraph that she is interested in showing how *Madison Avenue language has seeped into the funeral industry*, which means she's more interested in *how* the items are described than in the range of items available. Eliminate (A). While the descriptions might be funny, there's no evidence the author believes that the funeral industry intends to be funny, so eliminate (B). The issue of delaying decay is raised in some but not all of the examples, so eliminate (D) as not

addressing the examples overall. Choice (C) is consistent with the idea demonstrated by all of the examples, which do highlight the strangeness of describing funeral items in terms of benefits that the dead will never need. The correct answer is (C).

15. **C** This is a general question followed by a "best evidence" question, so treat the questions together as specific paired questions. Choice (16A) does not support any of the choices in question 15, so eliminate (16A). In the lines given in (16B), the author of passage 2 asserts *that in our search for economy and avoidance of discomfort we have weakened a very important family rite*. This works well to support (15C), so keep it. Choices (16C) and (16D) do provide examples of practices that the author raises questions about, but neither is an example of measures that are *ineffective* in addressing escalating funeral costs. Since (16C) and (16D) do not support any of the choices in question 15, they can be eliminated. The only answer choice in 15 that is supported by an answer in 16 is (15C). Eliminate (15A), (15B), and (15D). The correct answer for question 15 is (C), and the correct answer for question 16 is (B).

16. **B** See the explanation for question 15.

17. **A** The word *curbed* appears in the statement that *many of the questionable excesses of the funeral trade have been curbed*. This statement is followed by a colon and the explanation that *legislation and self-policing* have brought *some measure of regulation* to the funeral industry. Thus *curbed* must mean something like *reduced* or *made less excessive*. Eliminate (B), (C), and (D), which do not match this prediction. The correct answer is (A).

18. **D** The work for question 17 makes this question pretty straightforward to answer, since the phrase *questionable excesses of the funeral trade* appears in the lines that were used to answer question 17. The sentence explains that these excesses were curbed by *legislation and self-policing by funeral home associations*. Eliminate (A), (B), and (C), as these choices do not match the prediction; there's no reference to the *passage of time* as a factor, and, while the examples from (B) and (C) are mentioned in the passage, they do not address how the excesses were brought under control. The correct answer is (D).

19. **A** The author says to *Consider the case of one funeral "park"* that offers *drive-in funerals*. The example is provided to illustrate the claim made immediately before it that the *search for economy and avoidance of discomfort* have *weakened a very important family rite*. Choice (A) matches this prediction well. Eliminate (B), as it is not supported in the text and is a potentially offensive answer that a member of the funeral business is especially unlikely to make. The author does acknowledge that some positive changes have occurred in the funeral industry, but such changes are not being discussed in this paragraph. Eliminate (C). No claims that the funeral industry has not changed are mentioned in the passage, so the author is not *rebutting* them. Eliminate (D). The correct answer is (A).

20. **A** The referenced phrase occurs in the statement that *families will ask that contributions to charity be made in lieu of flowers and wreaths*, which is followed by the point that this occurs without the recognition *that buying flowers provides a chance for friends and relatives to show their concern in a*

more tangible way than a gift to charity. Since this opportunity to show tangible concern is not being acknowledged as important, friends and relatives must not have the opportunity to buy flowers and wreaths, so *in lieu of* must mean something like *instead of.* Eliminate (B), (C), and (D), as they do not match this prediction. Choice (A) is the correct answer.

21. **D**   The authors of both passages are most likely to agree on a point that each of them makes separately. Look at the answer choices so that you can look for support for the most likely candidate first. Choices (A) and (C) seem unlikely, as a member of the funeral industry is unlikely to make such strong claims, both of which are also inconsistent with the tone of the second passage. Choice (B) can also be eliminated, as the fact that the funeral industry has changed is essential to the argument made in the second passage. Choice (D) seems to be the most likely point upon which both authors agree, and evidence can be found in both passages when the information offered in the blurb is also considered—in the first passage because the author is writing about the negative aspects of the funeral industry in 1963, and in the second because the passage is from the 1980s and the author acknowledges that *many of the questionable excesses of the funeral trade have been curbed* in the last twenty years. Eliminate (A), (B), and (C). Choice (D) is the correct answer.

22. **D**   This general question is easier to answer after the more specific questions have been tackled. The passage begins by introducing the question of how life began and noting that numerous theories have been proposed to answer the question. Svante August Arrhenius's proposal is considered and the point is made that the solution ultimately leaves the central question unanswered. A second theory is introduced and Stanley Lloyd Miller's related experiment is described. Eliminate (A), as neither theory that is discussed is *proved to be impossible.* Eliminate (B), as it does not account for the discussion of the two theories. Eliminate (C), as the passage does not state that the question under consideration is *impossible to answer,* only one experiment is described, and that experiment is shown to *shed light* on the origin of life. Choice (D) best matches the prediction and is the correct answer.

23. **C**   The passage focuses on the question of how life on Earth arose, and since this occurred *perhaps 4,000 million years ago,* the larger details of the Earth's history prior to this point are less important than the details of what follows. Choices (A) and (B) present ideas that may be true but are not the primary reason the author does not feel the need to detail the earliest years of Earth's development too thoroughly. Eliminate (D) because while this aphorism may be true, it's not directly relevant to the choices the author makes in terms of how detailed the presented history is. Choice (C) matches the prediction well and is the correct answer.

24. **C**   The author presents Arrhenius's theory and then explains why, even if it is true, it still leaves open the question of how life began before it traveled to Earth. While Arrhenius's theory is described as *dramatic,* there is no evidence that the author thinks the theory is *innovative* or *daring,* so eliminate (A). Similarly, (B) can be eliminated, because while *dramatic* is supported, *too elaborate* is not. The author does not rule out the possibility that Arrhenius's theory is valid, so eliminate (D). The author chooses to highlight Arrhenius's theory from among several different theories that have been proposed, which suggests that the author finds the theory *interesting.* The phrase *even if we*

imagine that Earth was seeded from another world suggests that the author does not find the possibility particularly likely, however. Further, the author moves fairly quickly from Arrhenius's theory to another that is more fully elaborated on and that the author seems to find more relevant to the discussion, so the structure of the passage suggests that the author does not find Arrhenius's theory very likely. Choice (C) is best supported by the passage and is the correct answer.

25. **A** The word *generation* appears in the phrase *some period when life began on some world through spontaneous generation.* Since the passage is discussing how life arose from nonliving things, the thing that happens spontaneously must be the *creation or beginning of life.* Eliminate (C) and (D), as they refer to a different sense of the word *generation.* Eliminate (B) because if life did not yet exist, it could not be *reproduced,* only *produced.* Choice (A) matches the prediction and is the correct answer.

26. **D** The best evidence for the answer to an inference question is what the passage actually says on the topic. The second half of the sentence that notes that *Earth's atmosphere did not contain oxygen* is the explanation that the lack of oxygen also meant the absence of oxygen's derivative, ozone, and thus that *the Sun's energetic ultraviolet rays would reach Earth's surface undiluted.* Choice (A) might be true, but it does not identify the reason specifically given in the passage, so eliminate it. Choice (B) is extreme and there's no evidence that *all* energy sources produce more heat without oxygen, so eliminate it. Whether (C) is true or not, the issue it addresses is not discussed in the passage, so eliminate it, too. Choice (D) matches the prediction well and is the correct answer.

27. **A** Miller's experiment is discussed in the seventh paragraph and all the answer choices in question 28, a "best evidence" question, come from that paragraph, so the two questions can be treated as specific paired questions. The seventh paragraph opens with the claim that Miller made a discovery that *shed light on the passage from a substance that is definitely unliving to one that is, in however simple a fashion, alive.* This is another way of saying that Miller's discovery showed how life arose from nonliving substances. The paragraph's concluding sentence notes that Miller's work was *the first proof that organic material could have been formed from the inanimate substances.* Since that formation is the central concern of the passage as a whole, this is likely to be the reason the author discusses Miller's work. Choice (A) best fits with this prediction. Choices (B), (C), and (D) all touch on issues that may be relevant to the topic overall, but not as centrally as (A), which names the primary concern of the passage, so eliminate them. Choice (A) is the correct answer.

28. **A** This is the second question in a set of specific paired questions. The support for the answer in question 27 was found in the first and last sentences of the seventh paragraph. No answer choice covers the last sentence, but (A) does include the first sentence. Eliminate (B), (C), and (D). The correct answer is (A).

29. **C** The author's conclusion at the end of the passage is that Miller's experiment was *the first proof* that the conditions on Earth long ago could have been conducive to the spontaneous generation of life. The best support for the author's conclusion would also back up this *proof,* and that would entail either confirming or expanding upon Miller's findings. Choice (C) directly addresses that issue—if

Miller's results were duplicated by others, a conclusion based on Miller's work would be better supported. The other answer choices offer options that might generate interesting information, but they do not equally reinforce the evidence upon which the conclusion is based. Eliminate (A), (B), and (D). Choice (C) is the correct answer.

30. **B** This question asks which of the claims is supported by the table. Eliminate anything that isn't supported. Choice (A) can be eliminated because there is no evidence that any new amino acids were created in the twenty-first century. Choice (B) is supported by the table, so keep it. Choice (C) can be eliminated because only three of the first five amino acids found by Miller are proteinogenic. Choice (D) can be eliminated because the table shows eleven amino acids found by the Volcanic Spark Discharge experiment, and Miller-Urey found five. The correct answer is (B).

31. **B** This question asks which idea from the passage is most directly supported by the table. Choice (A) can be eliminated because the table contains data from an experiment testing the spontaneous generation of life on Earth, not the emergence of life from outer space. Choice (B) is supported, because Miller did apply an energy source to elements that existed on early Earth and found amino acids capable of building proteins. Keep (B). Choice (C) can be eliminated because the table does not show anything about the strength of the sun's rays. Choice (D) can be eliminated because there is nothing in the table about RNA. The correct answer is (B).

32. **A** This general question is easier to answer after the more specific questions have been tackled. The passage takes the form of an extended story that traces the author's actions upon reconsidering the author's response to a recently heard speaker. Choice (A) matches this prediction, so keep it. Eliminate (B), as the author ends up thinking that the symposium speaker's argument might have some validity after all, so the theory is not *debunked*. There is no introductory anecdote, as the entire passage is a story of the author's experiences and the thoughts they give rise to, so eliminate (C). The passage does not have a conclusion that *redefines the terms under discussion*, so eliminate (D). The correct answer is (A).

33. **A** The question asks for the author's *ultimate* attitude toward the symposium speaker, so this and question 34 can be treated as a set of specific paired questions, in which the answer to question 33 will probably be found in the latest mention of the speaker in the passage. (Alternatively, since the answer choices in 34 span the entire passage, these two questions could be worked as a set of general paired questions.) The latest reference to the symposium speaker—both in terms of the development of the author's attitudes and in the layout of the passage—comes in the last few lines of the passage: *And I'm starting to think that maybe the Whimsical Professor ranting about his "technological opiates" is not so romantic after all.* As before in the passage, the author gives the speaker a nickname that seems gently mocking but which also acknowledges some validity to the speaker's arguments. Choice (A) matches this prediction well. Eliminate (B), as there is no evidence the author is puzzled or feels a negative emotion as strong as scorn. Eliminate (C), since the author never rejected the speaker's ideas and there's no evidence the author dislikes the speaker. Eliminate (D), since the author does not exhibit a sense of nostalgia about the speaker or anything else in the passage. Choice (A) is the correct answer.

34. **D** Since this is the "best evidence" question that pairs with the specific question in 33, look for the answer choice in 34 that includes the lines that were used to predict the answer for 33. This refers to the last sentence of the passage, which is (D); the other three choices can be eliminated.

35. **C** This is a tricky question. Since it asks about the primary purpose of the details *In the context of the overall passage*, the correct answer is likely to be one that shows how those details contribute to the development of the main idea of the passage. Eliminate both (A) and (D), as these answers are more general and there is no indication in the answers of how *painting a picture in the reader's mind* or *evoking a sense of an idyllic college campus* would further the author's development of the main idea. Eliminate (B), since this explanation suggests that the author's main insight could be simply a product of a particular place rather than a generally applicable idea. Choice (C) suggests how the details in the first paragraph might contribute to the main idea overall, and even if it seems like a weak answer choice, it is more readily supported by the text than any other choice. The correct answer is (C).

36. **D** Consider the roles that punctuation and italics play in the referenced lines. Since there is no indication in line 9 that the quotation marks around *controversial* are intended to signal that the word is a quotation, the most likely explanation is that the author is using the term with reservation—that is, that the author did not actually think the symposium was actually controversial. This idea is reinforced by the summation, *I thought his speech was interesting, but altogether too romantic.* The second referenced line has a structure that suggests that two opposing ideas will be presented, as in a sentence like this: "They are never...sad either." Since the two ideas that are presented are actually the same phrase used twice, the italics are likely intended to indicate that the second use of the phrase *they are never alone* is different from the first. Eliminate (A) and (B), since the prediction provides a better explanation for the use of both quotation marks and italics than the need for *variation* or an *inconsistency.* Choice (C) also does not match the prediction, as there's no evidence that the author has a *whimsical* attitude toward the passage's main idea. Choice (D) matches the prediction and is the correct answer.

37. **D** The third paragraph is devoted to an account of the symposium speaker's argument. Eliminate (A), as the only details that relate to the speaker's *age and fatigue* come in the first sentence, so this answer doesn't account for the whole paragraph. Also eliminate (B), for while a contrast may exist between the speaker and the girls on their cell phones, the passage is devoted to detailing the speaker's ideas, not contrasting those ideas with the attitudes of the girls on their cell phones. Eliminate (C), as the author listened to the speaker in the morning and encountered the girls while eating lunch afterward, so the answer reverses the order of events. Choice (D) accounts for the whole paragraph, matches the prediction, and is the correct answer.

38. **B** When the task is to identify with which statement someone will most likely agree, the answer that repeats or rephrases something the person actually said will be the best supported choice. Check the answers against the comments that are attributed to the symposium speaker to see which best matches what the symposium speaker said. Eliminate (A), since there is no evidence the speaker distinguished between appropriate and inappropriate use of the icons. Eliminate (C) as extreme,

since the speaker does not make such a strong proclamation about the use of icons. Eliminate (D), since the speaker does not remark on the separate functions of dancing and flashing. Choice (B) is consistent with the speaker's assertion that a letter-writer had *time to think about his message* and *about how he could best phrase it*. The correct answer is (B).

39.　**B**　The beginning of the fourth paragraph—*And what about cell phones? I thought*—signals a transition from the summation of the symposium speaker's ideas to the author's own efforts to consider personal experiences in light of the speaker's larger claims. Eliminate (C) as there's no evidence the author believes people from a generation ago would not have tolerated the behavior. Eliminate (D), as there's no evidence the author believes a new etiquette book should be written. Eliminate (A), as this answer does not provide a connection to the ideas the speaker raised. Choice (B) matches the prediction and is the correct answer.

40.　**C**　The author's point in the referenced sentence is spelled out in the first sentence of the fifth paragraph: *those girls, like most of us, could use a moment of solitude*. The *significant price* the girls pay is that *they are never alone*, which, the author elaborates, contributes to the confused thinking that *being alone is the same thing as being lonely*. The author also asserts that *to disconnect* from the world for a while is necessary for *our sanity and identity as humans*. Eliminate (A), (B), and (D), as these are too literal interpretations of the downsides of using cell phones frequently, in public, and while doing other things. Choice (C) is most consistent with the prediction and is the correct answer.

41.　**B**　The *Whimsical Professor* is one of the nicknames the author bestows on the symposium speaker. The speaker's argument is summarized in the third paragraph, which offers the speaker's conclusion as *The temporary, impersonal nature of computers...is gradually rendering our lives equally temporary and impersonal*. The best counter to the speaker's claim would need to show why computers are not, in fact, rendering our own lives *equally temporary and impersonal*. Eliminate (A), as a speech with this title might actually reinforce the speaker's ideas. Eliminate (C), since no indication is given of how a speech with that title would address the issue of spelling nor that a decline in spelling standards makes our lives *temporary and impersonal*. Eliminate (D), since that title suggests that both sides of the debate will be addressed in a speech of that title; by contrast, the title in (B) clearly signals that the positive aspects of computer use will be discussed. Choice (B) matches the prediction by countering the speaker's negative conclusion with a positive thesis and is therefore the correct answer.

42.　**C**　The initial portrayal of the speaker, whose ideas are characterized by the author as *altogether too romantic*, suggests the speaker is out-of-step with the world around him—he is *antiquated*, wears mismatched clothes, rails *earnestly* against modern conveniences, and even uses the clunky-sounding *electronic mail* instead of its more common shorter form, email. By the end of the passage, when the term *romantic* is used again, the speaker has come to believe that the speaker is *not so romantic after all*, which reinforces the idea that the author uses *romantic* to mean not fully relevant or *not directly or practically applicable to current circumstances*. Eliminate (A), (B), and (D) as accepted definitions of *romantic* that do not fit this particular context. Choice (C) matches the prediction well and is the correct answer.

43.　**C**　This is a general question, and as such is probably easier to answer after the more specific questions have been tackled. The passage begins by asserting that few people *realize that certain events on the sun can have disastrous consequences* on Earth. After explaining how the events or CMEs can affect life on Earth, the passage addresses the difficulty in forecasting CMEs and how some on Earth are responding to the problems associated with them. Eliminate (A), as the passage does not *detail* the positive effects of CMEs. While the passage does say that CME is the term used by scientists to denote solar projections, it does not explain the phenomenon twice using two different kinds of terms; eliminate (B). There's no evidence in the passage that CMEs are *new* or that the author is issuing a warning, so eliminate (D). Choice (C) matches the prediction well and is the correct answer.

44.　**C**　The indicated phrase occurs in the first paragraph in a sentence that might require a little untangling. The sentence that immediately follows the referenced line can provide useful context, as it is more straightforward: *Few people realize, however, that certain events on the sun can have disastrous consequences for life here on Earth.* The *however* indicates that the idea that the sun can have disastrous effects on Earth contrasts with the information provided in the first sentence, so the first sentence must indicate that people don't usually think the sun affects the Earth adversely. This suggests that the phrase *almost unambiguously benign* refers to the opinion most people have of the effects of the sun on Earth. Eliminate (B) and (D), as neither addresses the issue of what people think of the sun. When (A) and (C) are compared, (C) is the stronger answer that better matches the prediction; (A) incorporates a misreading of the phrase *on the surface*, which in the context of the passage means *at first glance* and does not literally refer to Earth's surface. Eliminate (A). The correct answer is (C).

45.　**B**　This question is a general question that is followed by a "best evidence" question whose answer choices are drawn from the whole of the passage, so questions 45 and 46 can be worked as a set of general paired questions. Choice (46A) does address the issue of how many people know about the potential that CMEs have to cause problems on Earth, but the indicated lines do not address governmental plans. Eliminate (46A) or mark its connection to (45A) as weak. Choice (46B) explicitly connects increasing dependence on new technologies to an increase in the potential havoc a major CME could cause. This answer offers strong support for (45B). Choice (46C) explains what scientists conjecture about a *perfect storm*, but the author does not draw attention to any ironies that might exist in the application of the term; thus while (46C) might offer some support to (45D), the support is not as strong as that offered by (46B) for (45B). Eliminate (46C). Choice (46D) does explain the high speeds at which CMEs travel, but there is no indication the author believes the difficulties caused by such speeds will not be overcome at any point in the future. Eliminate (46D). Eliminate (45A), (45C), and (45D), as none is as well-supported as (45B) is by (46B). The correct answer for question 45 is (B), and the correct answer for question 46 is (B).

46.　**B**　See the explanation for the previous question.

47.   **D**   The term *geomagnetic storm* can be used as a lead word to locate the introduction of that term in line 6; CMEs are explained later in the first paragraph, so look there to see which answer choice is supported by the passage. There is no mention of the frequency of either phenomenon, so eliminate (A). The relationship between DST and CMEs is not addressed, so eliminate (B). The passage does not clarify if the relative size of plasma ejections affects which term is applied when, so eliminate (C). The passage explains that CMEs are ejections of plasma from the sun's surface and the first sentence of the second paragraph refers to the *last...major CME* and explains the effects of *the resulting geomagnetic storm*. These details are consistent with the explanation offered in (D). Thus, the correct answer is (D).

48.   **D**   The words *compounded by* occur in the following phrase: *The difficulties created by this narrow window of opportunity are compounded by the fact that....* The rest of the sentence goes on to describe a second factor that severely limits the time scientists have to analyze and formulate responses to a major CME. Thus *compounded by* must mean something like *complicated by* or *made even more difficult by*. Eliminate (A) and (B), which do not match the prediction at all, and (C), which does not match the prediction as well as (D) does. Choice (D) is the correct answer.

49.   **C**   Chronology and the use of *governments* as a lead word help to locate the reference to how some *world governments hope to combat this problem by placing a satellite in orbit around the sun* at the start of the final paragraph. The previous paragraph describes the challenges of trying to predict a geomagnetic storm's impact, so the problem the governments want to use a satellite to combat is the problem specified in the question. Eliminate (A) and (B), as these options do not match the prediction and are not discussed anywhere in the passage. Eliminate (D) because while the attempted solutions described are mentioned in the passage, these are steps taken—by *energy providers*—to minimize the effects of a CME, not steps taken to provide more time in which to analyze and respond to a CME. Choice (C) matches the prediction and is the correct answer.

50.   **A**   The word *buy* occurs in the phrase *in the hopes that this will buy scientists more time to predict the occurrence and intensity of geomagnetic storms*. Since a major difficulty with geomagnetic storms is the very short window in which scientists can try to analyze a CME once it occurs, the benefit of placing a satellite in orbit around the sun would be that data about the CME would be available earlier in that window. Thus in this context, *buy* must mean something like *offer to* or *gain*. Eliminate (C) as it is not relevant in this context. Eliminate (D) as a too literal definition of *buy* that also does not fit in this context. Between (A) and (B), (A) better matches the prediction, while (B) introduces a suggestion of *deserving* or *being entitled to* that does not suit the context as well. Eliminate (B). The correct answer is (A).

51.   **D**   The question asks for the answer that is *consistent with information in the passage and the graph*, so check the answer choices to determine which one doesn't contradict the passage and graph. Choice (A) might initially seem consistent with the graph, since the year 2001 features the highest plotted point on the graph (at −10). The start of the second paragraph, however, refers to the *last recorded instance of a major CME*, which *occurred in 1989* and resulted in a geomagnetic storm that caused very large-scale problems. Furthermore, if 1989 contained such a significant CME,

then it seems very unlikely that a relatively high value on the vertical axis signals a great deal of geomagnetic storm activity. Eliminate (A), since the last major CME occurred in 1989, not 2001. Eliminate (B), since lower, not higher, relative values on the vertical axis seem to indicate greater geomagnetic storm activity. Eliminate (C), as the start of the third paragraph notes that *perfect storms*, or storms with the potential to cause massive disruptions on Earth, are *difficult to forecast*, so the graph is unlikely to provide any basis for making a prediction about when the next major CME would occur. Choice (D) is consistent with the passage and graph, which together suggest an inverse relationship between DST measure and the strength of geomagnetic storm activity. Choice (D) is the correct answer.

52. **A** The question asks which statement is best supported by the data in the graph, so look for an answer choice that agrees with or at least does not contradict the graph. Choice (A) is consistent with the apparently random pattern of activity that the graph shows, so keep it. Choice (B), like (A), paraphrases information provided in the passage; however, the speed of CMEs is not addressed by the graph, so eliminate (B). The graph also does not support the extreme claim made in (C), nor does it address the factors that result in a storm causing damage. Eliminate (C). Choice (D) also paraphrases information given in the passage, but the timeframe for determining the orientation of a CME's magnetic field is not addressed by the graph. Eliminate (D). Choice (A) is the correct answer.

Chapter 6
Writing and
Language

GRAMMAR

Quick—identify the correlative conjunction in the nonrestrictive clause in the following sentence:

1. Just kidding!

You can relax now; the grammar tested on the SAT is not going to be that difficult. Instead, the Writing and Language section requires you to know only a few basic rules. The SAT will test these rules with two basic types of questions: Proofreader questions and Editor questions.

Proofreader Questions

Proofreader questions on the SAT look like this.

The history of **1** language although it may sound like a boring subject, is a treasure trove of historical, cultural, and psychological insights.

1

A) NO CHANGE
B) language, although it may sound like a boring subject
C) language, although it may sound, like a boring subject,
D) language, although it may sound like a boring subject,

Most students make the mistake of reading the sentence four times, with each of the answers substituted in, and trying to figure out what sounds wrong. However, this is not a very safe or efficient way of tackling these problems. Notice how all of the answers are virtually identical. The ONLY difference is in the placement of commas. So, rather than reading the sentence over and over again, go straight to the answers! Ask yourself, "What's changing?" (In case you're curious, (D) is the answer.)

Note that these questions don't generally have an actual question, and about 25 percent of them will require "NO CHANGE."

Editor Questions

Editor questions on the SAT look like this.

The problem has certainly gained a good deal of traction in public debates. **2**

A decade of gridlock within the legislature has prevented many needed reforms from moving forward.

2

At this point, the writer is considering adding the following sentence.

> This raises the question of why more isn't being done to combat the gap.

Should the writer make this addition here?

A) Yes, because it adds specific details about the gap mentioned earlier in the paragraph.

B) Yes, because it raises a question that is answered in the next paragraph.

C) No, because it repeats an idea already stated earlier in the paragraph.

D) No, because it is not relevant to the public debates.

While Proofreader questions have an implied question, Editor questions actually have a question stem. This one asks whether a sentence should be added. Choice (B) is the correct answer because the added sentence connects the ideas in the two paragraphs. The sentence doesn't add any specific details, so the answer can't be (A). It doesn't appear to be repetitive, so the answer can't be (C), and it is drawing a contrast between the public debates and the legislature, so the answer can't be (D).

Graphs

No, this isn't the Math section, but you'll see a graph or other figure on at least one passage in the Writing and Language section. Apply the same approach to figures in this section that you use in the Reading and Math sections: that is, read the labels on the figures carefully, and use POE. In the Writing and Language section, eliminate answer choices that aren't consistent with the data, but also pay attention to whether the graph is relevant to the subject of the passage.

Graph questions on the SAT Writing and Language section look like this.

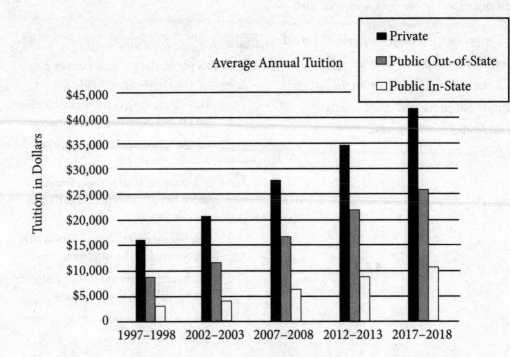

Average Annual Tuition

Many families are increasingly concerned about paying for college, and with good reason: tuition rates have been steadily rising for many years. Over the past decade, **3** tuition has increased at a much higher rate than need-based grants have.

3

Which choice provides the most accurate interpretation of the figure?

A) NO CHANGE

B) out-of-state tuition at public schools has risen to be equal to private school tuition.

C) the average tuition at all types of schools has more than doubled.

D) tuition at public schools has risen so much that it has become unaffordable for many families.

Read the labels on the figure. The title tells you that the figure shows "Average Annual Tuition," and the key shows that the different bars on the graph are different types of schools. The x-axis shows academic year, and the y-axis shows dollars. The graph does not give any information about *need-based grants* or whether school is *unaffordable*, so eliminate (A) and (D). Tuition has risen at all three types of schools shown, but out-of-state public-school tuition is less than private school tuition in all years, so eliminate (B). All three types have more than doubled over the decade shown, so choose (C).

THE PRINCETON REVIEW METHOD

Step One

Familiarize yourself with the most commonly tested grammatical errors. The SAT tests only a handful of errors. Once you learn these rules and become comfortable with them, keep your eyes peeled for them on the test.

Step Two

Make aggressive use of Process of Elimination. If you're not sure what the right answer is, find and eliminate any answers you know are wrong.

COMMON GRAMMATICAL ERRORS

Transition Words

When the SAT underlines a transition, it's testing whether you can choose the word that appropriately links the sentences that come before and after the transition. In other words, you should look for a transition that is *consistent* with the ideas it connects. Here is a list of some common transitions.

Keeps the ideas similar:	*Shows a contrast:*
And	Although / Though / Even though
Since	However
In fact	Yet
Therefore	But
Thus	Rather
So	In contrast to
Also	Despite
As well as	Unlike
Moreover	Instead
Consequently	Nevertheless
Hence	Nonetheless
Finally	Notwithstanding
Subsequently	Alternatively
In addition	
Likewise	

Try this example.

Dark chocolate contains less sugar and fewer calories than milk chocolate does. **4** Additionally, because it contains more antioxidants, it may help to prevent heart disease.

4
A) NO CHANGE
B) However,
C) Although,
D) For example,

It sounds like dark chocolate is pretty wonderful, right? Less sugar and fewer calories are both positive things. Reading what comes after the conjunction, you see that dark chocolate also contains antioxidants that may prevent heart disease, another positive. You need something that keeps the flow of ideas similar. Both (B) and (C) would indicate a shift or contrast, so eliminate them. The second sentence does not contain an example of the idea in the first sentence, so eliminate (D) as well, and you're left with the correct answer, (A).

Quick Quiz 1

Although the triathlon is the most popular multi-event sport, there are numerous others that most people are unaware of. **1** Rather, the biathlon—a winter sport that combines cross-country skiing and rifle shooting—is almost unknown to the general public.

1
A) NO CHANGE
B) In contrast,
C) For example,
D) However,

The forecast calls for rain this weekend. **2** Although, we do not plan to cancel our trip to the zoo.

2
A) NO CHANGE
B) However,
C) Moreover,
D) On the contrary,

After weeks of rain and storms, the tourist board began to worry. **3** Otherwise, no one likes to visit during bad weather, and no tourists means less tax revenue.

3
A) NO CHANGE
B) Therefore,
C) Nevertheless,
D) After all,

Answers and Explanations: Quick Quiz 1

1. **C** The question is testing **transitions,** so first determine how the ideas are connected. The first sentence discusses sports that *most people are unaware of* and the second sentence says that the biathlon is *almost unknown,* so the ideas are similar. The transitions *Rather, In contrast,* and *However* all indicate opposite ideas, so eliminate them. *For example* indicates more of the same, so (C) is the correct answer.

2. **B** The question is testing **transitions,** so first determine how the ideas are connected. The idea of *rain* and deciding *not…to cancel* the trip are opposite ideas. *Moreover* indicates the same direction, so eliminate (C). *Although* is used to connect opposite ideas in the same sentence, but here the opposite idea is in the previous sentence, so it doesn't work. Eliminate (A). *On the contrary* is used to argue against the previous idea, but going to the zoo does not refute that it will rain, so eliminate (D). *However* correctly links the two opposite ideas, so (B) is the correct answer.

3. **D** The question is testing **transitions,** so first determine how the ideas are connected. The first sentence states that the *tourist board began to worry* and the second sentence states why they worried, so the two ideas are similar. *Otherwise* and *Nevertheless* indicate opposite ideas, so eliminate (A) and (C). *Therefore* indicates that the second sentence is a consequence of the first; this is backwards, so eliminate (B). *After all* indicates that the second sentence is the reason for the first, which makes (D) the correct answer.

Verb Errors

When you see a verb underlined, check to make sure it is **consistent with its subject.** Also, make sure that verbs are **consistent in tense** with the rest of the sentence or paragraph.

Quick Quiz 2

Last year, as in years past, the majority of candidates **1** are dropping out of the race before the actual election because they no longer had the funds or the will to campaign.

1

A) NO CHANGE
B) is dropping
C) dropped
D) drop

Restrictions on one of the committees that **2** monitors corporate waste disposal were revoked, allowing the committee to levy fines on violators of the disposal laws.

2

A) NO CHANGE
B) monitor
C) monitoring
D) will monitor

3 The Lipizzaner, a breed of horses that nearly went extinct at the end of World War II, are featured in performances at the Hofburg Palace in Vienna.

3

A) NO CHANGE
B) The Lipizzaner, a breed of horses that nearly went extinct at the end of World War II, is
C) Lipizzaners, a breed of horses that nearly went extinct at the end of World War II, is
D) The Lipizzaner, a breed of horses that nearly went extinct at the end of World War II; as such it is

Answers and Explanations: Quick Quiz 2

1. **C** The sentence is in the past **tense**, as indicated by *last year*. Choices (A), (B), and (D) are wrong because they are in the present tense.

2. **A** The question is testing **consistency,** so find the subject of the verb. The verb *monitors* is singular, while *one* of the committees, the subject of the verb, is also singular. Note that prepositional phrases such as *of the committees* are almost always irrelevant and are designed to trick your ear. A prepositional phrase can't be the subject of a verb, so when you see a preposition, look before it to find the subject.

3. **B** The question is testing **consistency,** so find the subject of the verb. The subject in the original is *Lipizzaner*, which takes a singular verb but is paired here with *are*. Eliminate (A). Choice (C) changes the verb from *are* to *is*, but it also changes the subject from *The Lipizzaner* to *Lipizzaners*, which makes for an incorrect subject-verb pairing. Eliminate (C). Choice (D) has the right subject-verb pairing but incorrectly introduces a semicolon, so eliminate (D). Choice (B) is the correct answer, as it pairs *The Lipizzaner* with *is* and the singular subject is consistent with the phrase *a breed* that refers back to it.

Pronoun Errors

Pronouns are one of the College Board's favorite grammar subjects to test. When you see a pronoun underlined, check to see if it is **consistent** with the noun it replaces. Don't be fooled by your ear when dealing with pronouns on the SAT. It's common in everyday speech to use the pronouns they, them, and their to refer to a singular person of unspecified gender, but on the SAT those pronouns are *always* plural. Don't worry—you won't have to choose a gendered pronoun if it's at all unclear what the gender is.

Here's a table of the pronouns you're most likely to see on the SAT.

	1st person	2nd person	3rd person
Singular	I, me, my, mine	you, your, yours	she, he, it, her, him, hers, his, its
Plural	we, us, our, ours	you, your, yours	they, them, their, theirs

Remember: The following pronouns are always singular:

- Any pronoun ending in –one (anyone, someone, everyone)
- Any pronoun ending in –body (anybody, nobody, somebody)
- Any pronoun ending in –thing (anything, nothing, something)
- The pronoun *each*

Another way in which your ear can lead you astray with pronouns is when there are contractions. Do you know the difference between *its* and *it's*? Or *their* and *they're*? When a pronoun has an apostrophe, it's a contraction. *It's* means *it is*, whereas *its* is a possessive pronoun. Similarly, *they're* means *they are*, while *their* is a possessive pronoun. And to make *their/they're* even more confusing, there's also *there*, which isn't a pronoun at all, but is used to indicate location.

When you see *it's/its* or *they're/their/there* in the answer choices, your ear won't help—they sound the same! So be sure to know the different functions of these words so you can choose the correct one for the context.

Also check pronouns for **ambiguity**. The following sentence is grammatically incorrect:

> *Successful athletes pay attention to their coaches because they know the value of experience.*

Who does *they* refer to, the coaches or the athletes? If you can't tell, then the pronoun is ambiguous, and you should replace it with a noun.

Quick Quiz 3

If the company continues to lose customers to **1** their competitors, the stock price of the company will continue to fall.

1

A) NO CHANGE
B) our
C) its
D) one's own

Many photographers are coming to believe that color prints are as artistic as black and white ones because **2** these reveal new definitions of art.

2

A) NO CHANGE
B) they reveal
C) it reveals
D) color prints reveal

The Africanized honey bee is so aggressive that **3** its better known by its colloquial name: killer bee.

3

A) NO CHANGE
B) it's
C) their
D) they're

While many cooking experts hold that the only proper way to bake a potato is in a conventional oven, others contend that cooking **4** them in a microwave is a perfectly acceptable alternative.

4

A) NO CHANGE
B) it
C) they
D) those

If changing the policy were as easy as signing **5** there names to the petition, the members could have stopped protesting months ago.

5

A) NO CHANGE
B) its
C) their
D) they're

Answers and Explanations: Quick Quiz 3

1. **C** The issue here is **pronoun consistency.** The underlined refers to *the company*, which is singular. The correct answer is (C) because it is a singular pronoun that is consistent with *the company*.

2. **D** This is a **pronoun ambiguity** question because *these* and *they* could refer to photographers, color prints, or black and white prints. Only (D) clarifies this ambiguity. The subject is plural, so *it* is not consistent.

3. **B** The issue is both **pronoun consistency** and **apostrophes.** The pronoun refers to the singular *honey bee,* so eliminate (C) and (D). The sentence is saying that *it is better known,* so an apostrophe is needed for the contraction. The correct answer is (B).

4. **B** Remember to check pronouns for **consistency** with the nouns they replace. The pronoun *them* (plural) refers to the noun *potato* (singular). You can NEVER mix a singular with a plural. The singular form you need is *it*.

5. **C** The issue is both **pronoun consistency** and **apostrophes.** The pronoun refers to the *members*, which is plural, and the *names* belong to the *members*, so the plural possessive pronoun is needed. *Their* is the plural possessive, so (C) is the correct answer.

Now let's take a closer look at some other grammar issues that you will be sure to see in Writing and Language questions.

PUNCTUATION

When you are linking multiple ideas in the same sentence, be sure to use the appropriate punctuation.

STOP	HALF-STOP	GO
• Period	• Colon	• Comma
• Semicolon	• Long dash	• No punctuation
• Comma + FANBOYS		
• Question mark		
• Exclamation Mark		

FANBOYS stands for **F**or, **A**nd, **N**or, **B**ut, **O**r, **Y**et, and **S**o.

> STOP punctuation can link *only* complete ideas.
>
> HALF-STOP punctuation must be *preceded* by a complete idea.
>
> GO punctuation can link anything *except* two complete ideas.

Jonah, the valedictorian of his senior class, believes that only one factor contributed to his success in **1** school; his commitment to hard work.

1

A) NO CHANGE

B) school; and it was

C) school:

D) school, being

As always, check what's changing in the answer choices. In this case, the words vary somewhat, but notice the types of punctuation that are changing: STOP, HALF-STOP, and GO.

When you see different types of punctuation in the answer choices, you can use what we call the Vertical Line Test to help you determine which type of punctuation to use.

Here's how the Vertical Line Test works: draw a line where you see the punctuation changing—in this case, between the words *school* and *his*. Then, read up to the vertical line: *Jonah...believes that only one factor contributed to his success in school*. That's complete. Now, read after the vertical line: *his commitment to hard work*. That's NOT complete.

If there aren't two compete ideas, you can't use STOP punctuation. Eliminate (A) and (B). Either HALF-STOP or GO punctuation could work here, but in (D), the word *being* is unnecessary and wordy. Eliminate (D); (C) is the correct answer.

Try another.

It was a top priority for Jonah to do well in **2** school; though his love of friends, family, and sports were just as important.

2

A) NO CHANGE
B) school, but his
C) school; and his
D) school, his

Check the answer choices. What's changing? Punctuation, and also words. Sometimes, changing words in a sentence changes ideas from complete to incomplete or vice versa. Since the punctuation is changing, start by using the Vertical Line Test.

Draw a vertical line after *school*. The first part of the sentence is a complete idea. As it's written, the second part of the sentence (*though his love…*) is an incomplete idea. You can't have STOP punctuation between a complete and an incomplete idea, so eliminate (A).

Choices (B) and (C) both have FANBOYS. Since *but* in (B) is preceded by a comma, that means it has STOP punctuation. Both parts of the sentence are complete in this case, so (B) works. Eliminate (C) because the combination of a semicolon, which is STOP punctuation, and FANBOYS is overkill. Choice (D) has GO punctuation, but in this case, since the word *though* from the original sentence has been removed, both parts of the sentence are complete. GO punctuation can't be used between two complete ideas, so eliminate (D). The correct answer is (B).

Try one more.

Admittedly, advanced planning and time management, two necessary characteristics of high **3** achievers, have also been the cornerstones of Jonah's high school success story.

A) NO CHANGE
B) achievers—
C) achievers;
D) achievers:

The punctuation is changing in the answer choices, and there's some STOP punctuation, so use the Vertical Line Test. Put the line between *achievers* and *have*. The first idea, *Admittedly, advanced planning and time management, two necessary characteristics of high achievers*, is incomplete, and the second idea, *have also been the cornerstones of Jonah's high school success story* is also incomplete. Therefore, you can't use STOP (which needs two complete ideas) or HALF-STOP (which needs a complete idea before the punctuation), thus eliminating (B), (C), and (D). Choice (A) is the correct answer.

COMMAS

On the SAT, there are only four reasons to use a comma:

- in STOP punctuation, with one of the FANBOYS
- in GO punctuation, to separate incomplete ideas from other ideas
- in a list of three or more things
- in a sentence containing unnecessary information

If you can't cite a reason to use a comma, *don't use one.*

We've already seen the first two concepts, so let's look at the other two.

Try this one.

Environmentalists, **4** consumers; and government officials are all working together to develop new solutions to pollution problems.

4

A) NO CHANGE
B) consumers: and
C) consumers, and
D) consumers, and,

First, check what's changing in the answer choices. It looks like punctuation is changing. You may be tempted to use the Vertical Line Test here, but there's one little exception to be aware of: a comma followed by FANBOYS at the end of a list does NOT act as STOP punctuation. So rule out (A) and (B).

The rule you need to know here is that the SAT expects a comma after every item in a series of three or more items. That's because there is a potential for ambiguity when this punctuation isn't used.

I went to the park with my parents, my cat Violet and my dog Stuart.

If there's no comma, how do you know that this sentence isn't supposed to mean that the parents are *my cat Violet and my dog Stuart*? The only way to clear things up is to add a comma before the word *and*.

I went to the park with my parents, my cat Violet, and my dog Stuart.

Keep that in mind as you work number 4. In this problem, *Environmentalists, consumers, and government officials* form a list of three items, so they should be separated by commas. Eliminate (A) and (B) because they don't have commas. There's no need for a comma after *and*, so eliminate (D) also. The correct answer is (C).

Try another.

5 Jonah, the valedictorian of his senior class believes that only one factor contributed to his success in school: his commitment to hard work.

5

A) NO CHANGE

B) Jonah the valedictorian of his senior class,

C) Jonah, the valedictorian of his senior class,

D) Jonah, the valedictorian, of his senior class

First, check what's changing in the answer choices. Just commas, so the Vertical Line Test will not help here. There's no list in the sentence, so that rule doesn't apply, but notice how commas seem to be circling around the words *the valedictorian of his senior class*. When you have a few commas circling around a word, phrase, or clause like this, the question is usually testing the unnecessary information comma rule.

A good way to determine whether an idea is necessary to the meaning of the sentence is to take it out. Read the original sentence again, and check whether the sentence is still complete and retains the intended meaning. Read this one without the potentially unnecessary phrase: *Jonah believes that only one factor contributed to his success in school: his commitment to hard work.*

Is the sentence still complete? Yes. Has the meaning of the sentence changed? No, it just lost an extra detail. Therefore, the idea is *unnecessary* to the meaning of the sentence and should be set off with commas as it is in (C). Choice (D) has an extra comma, while neither (A) nor (B) has enough commas.

These last two examples both had commas in the correct answer, but remember: if you can't find a reason to use a comma, pick the answer choice that doesn't have any!

APOSTROPHES

As with commas, if you can't cite a reason to use an apostrophe, don't use one. There are only two reasons to use apostrophes on the SAT:

- Possessive nouns (NOT pronouns)
- Contractions

Here are some examples.

Commercial farming often results in excess fertilizer use, which **6** can pollute nearby ponds, resulting in an overgrowth of algae.

6

A) NO CHANGE
B) can pollute nearby pond's,
C) could have polluted nearby ponds,
D) has polluted nearby pond's,

Check what's changing in the answer choices. There are a few shifts in tense, but the apostrophes are also changing. Remember: if you can't cite a reason to use an apostrophe, don't use one.

Does anything belong to *ponds*? No! Is this supposed to be a contraction, like *pond is?* No! Therefore, there's no reason to use an apostrophe, so eliminate (B) and (D). Choice (C) changes the tense, and thus the meaning, of the sentence, so it's also wrong, leaving (A) as the correct answer.

In this case, the SAT is testing whether you can spot unnecessary punctuation. Sometimes the test will check the opposite: that is, when apostrophes are necessary.

The first time I visited the museum, I couldn't wait to view a specific **7** painters work, Andrew Wyeth's *Christina's World.*

7

A) NO CHANGE
B) painter's work;
C) painters work
D) painter's work:

Check what's changing in the answer choices. The main changes have to do with apostrophes and other punctuation.

Painter's needs an apostrophe: the work belongs to the painter. Eliminate (A) and (C). As for the punctuation, use the Vertical Line Test. The first part of the sentence, up through *work* is a complete idea, but the second part, starting with *Andrew Wyeth's,* is an incomplete idea. You can't use STOP punctuation if there aren't two complete ideas, so eliminate (B). Choose (D).

NUANCES

The SAT will also test a few other things that have more to do with word choice than with grammar. If you don't spot a pronoun, verb, or punctuation error, check for the following.

Idioms

Idioms are specific arrangements of words that convey a certain meaning. For example, the phrase *responsible for* is an idiom; you wouldn't say *responsible of.* If you see a preposition underlined, check to see if it's used idiomatically.

Precision

Precision errors are errors in word choice. These are not hard to spot, because you will see single words with similar meanings. Your job is to choose the word that gives the most **precise** meaning to the sentence.

> For a specific list of tricky words and phrases to look out for, please see the Appendix on Prepositions and Idioms at the back of the book.

Frequently Confused Words

Than is used for comparison (greater *than*, less *than*).
Then is used for time (and *then* we went to the library).

Affect is generally used as a verb (the change will *affect* all the students).
Effect is generally used as a noun (the students will feel the *effects* of the change).

Concision

If you were to ask for directions, which answer would you rather receive?

Turn right at Main Street and walk four blocks.

or

Since this street, Elm Street, is facing in a northerly direction, and your destination is due north-east, go east when you arrive at the intersection of Elm and Main. Going east will entail making a right turn in quite that easterly direction. After having made this turn and arrived on the perpendicular street….

The first one is obviously preferable. That's because concision is key when you want to communicate meaning. Really, as long as everything else is in order—as long as the grammar and punctuation are good to go—the best answer will almost always be the shortest.

Here's an example.

The warming trend environmentalists observed in the 1990s may repeat [8] itself again, with harmful long-term effects on various species throughout the planet.

[8]
A) NO CHANGE
B) itself,
C) itself, with much damage and
D) itself possibly,

You may immediately be drawn to (B) because it is the most concise choice. Before you pick (B) though, look at the other words in the answers and decide if they add any important details to the sentence. In (A), *again* is simply an echo of the word *repeat*, just as in (D), *possibly*, is a rehash of *may*, so eliminate both. In (C), *damage* is unnecessary, as the sentence already contains the word *harmful*. Choose (B).

Common Editor Questions to Look Out For

Here is one type of Editor question (that is, it actually has a question) that shows up on every test.

Although Tyson claimed his company's main concern was helping people, it was later revealed that his priority was making money. [9]

[9]
The writer wants to add detail to support the claim made in the previous sentence. Which choice best accomplishes this goal?

A) Tyson became a millionaire at the age of 26 when he inherited his father's fortune.

B) Despite thousands of consumer complaints over the past 5 years, the company grew 350%, making huge profits.

C) Although many people were hurt by the company, most of them still approve of Tyson's work.

D) No one can make that much money without cutting corners and manipulating the system.

The question asks for a detail that supports the claim. In this case, the detail must address *making money* while not *helping people*. Both (A) and (D) discuss the money but do not address whether people were helped or hurt in order to get the money, so they're not correct. Choice (C) doesn't address making money at all, so it's out. Choice (B) addresses both points, so it's the best supporting detail and the correct answer.

Here is another common question type.

The gender disparities persist in areas other than pay. It is a kind of open secret, for instance, that women have had the right to vote in the United States for less than a century. **10** There is a long history of misogyny written into the very cultural and social fabric of the United States.

10

At this point, the writer is considering adding the following true statement:

> The year that women's suffrage became legal in the United States was also the year that the American Football League was formed under the leadership of Jim Thorpe.

Should the writer make this addition here?

A) Yes, because it gives a broader context to the achievement of women's suffrage.

B) Yes, because it helps to ease some of the political rhetoric in the rest of the passage.

C) No, because it does not contribute in a significant way to the discussion of the gender pay gap.

D) No, because the question of gender pay is irrelevant when all football players are men.

The proposed sentence does contain an interesting bit of information, but that piece of information has no clear place either in these few sentences or in the passage as a whole. Therefore, it should not be added, thus eliminating (A) and (B).

Then, because it does not play a significant role in the passage, the sentence should not be added for the reason stated in (C). While (D) may be true in a way, it does not reflect anything clearly relating to the role the sentence might play in the passage as a whole. Read literally, and answer as literally and precisely as you can.

Quick Quiz 4

Clothing can be made from many different types of substances. There are two main groups of fibers: natural and man-made. Some natural fibers are cotton, wool, and linen, and some man-made fibers are polyester, rayon, and nylon; the difference depends on look and feel.

Many people prefer to wear natural fibers because they feel more **1** happy against the skin. The wearer perspires less because the organic cloth breathes.

2 Unlike natural fabrics, man-made fabrics wrinkle less, but they do not feel as pleasant on the body. Artificial fibers tend to make a person sweat more because they are composed of a plastic base. Plastic does not breathe very well; think of a plastic rain poncho. But because plastic is man-made, it is easier to manipulate than natural cloth. Because we don't like wrinkly clothes, we make artificial fabrics that stay and remain wrinkle-free. Because we don't like wrinkly clothes, we make artificial fabrics that **3** stay and remain wrinkle-free so that our clothes don't get rumpled.

[1] So if one wants to look ironed and crisp all day, wear man-made clothes. [2] But if one prefers the comfort and feel of aeration and a perspiration-free feeling, choose natural fibers. [3] Determining whether you're a style or a texture person determines which fabrics you'll prefer. [4] If you cannot decide, try a blend! **4**

1

A) NO CHANGE
B) comfortable
C) relaxed
D) easy

2

Which choice provides the most effective transition from the previous paragraph?

A) NO CHANGE
B) Cotton and linen are not man-made fibers and, consequently, behave differently.
C) Nevertheless, all fibers have their advantages, especially man-made fibers.
D) Some fibers encourage perspiration, a healthy, cleansing process of the skin.

3

A) NO CHANGE
B) stay wrinkle-free and keep our clothes smooth.
C) keep wrinkles out of our clothes because the fabrics don't rumple.
D) remain wrinkle-free.

4

To make this paragraph most logical, sentence 3 should be placed

A) where it is now.
B) before sentence 1.
C) before sentence 2.
D) after sentence 4.

Answers and Explanations: Quick Quiz 4

1. **B** This question is testing **precision**. The words in the answer choices could be synonyms, but there are slight nuances in meaning that make (A), (C), and (D) all not work in this context. Choice (B) gives the most precise meaning in context.

2. **A** For **transition** questions, go back to the passage and read the sentences before and after the one you're going to work with. Determine what direction the sentences are going in—do they maintain the same flow of ideas or does the topic change from one sentence to the next? When adding a transition, do not go off-topic or add any new information. The end of the second paragraph discusses a benefit of natural fibers. The start of the third paragraph addresses artificial fibers. Since this marks a change of direction, look for the choice that addresses this topic shift. Choice (A) serves as an effective transition between the characteristics of natural fibers and those of artificial fibers. Choice (A) is correct.

3. **D** The issue here is **concision**. All of the choices mean basically the same thing, but (D) is correct because it says it in the fewest words. The other choices are long and redundant, repeating the idea of *wrinkle-free* many times.

4. **B** This question asks for the best placement for sentence 3. Look for other sentences that are **consistent** with the ideas in sentence 3. Sentence 3 introduces two considerations for choosing a fabric: style and texture. Sentences 1 and 2 expand on those two ideas, so sentence 3 should come before sentence 1. The correct answer is (B).

Now that you've learned all the rules, try some of these Problem Sets.

PROOFREADER PROBLEM SET 1

If Charlie saved just 10% of his income, he could reach his retirement goal. **1** So, he continues to throw his money away buying lottery tickets.

1

A) NO CHANGE
B) Therefore,
C) However,
D) Fortunately,

The well-manicured lawns, the marble columns, and the impressive fountains indicated that this was no **2** ordinary summer cottage.

2

A) NO CHANGE
B) established
C) daily
D) customary

Considering the blinding snowstorm and ice-covered roads, she **3** have been lucky to arrive here safely.

3

A) NO CHANGE
B) were
C) has been
D) was

This most recent documentary contains many examples illustrating how corrupt the political system of the 1920s **4** is.

4

A) NO CHANGE
B) has been
C) were
D) was

Eager to reach the widest audience possible, the popular group ABBA recorded songs not only in 5 their native Swedish but also in a number of other languages.

5
A) NO CHANGE
B) they're
C) its
D) it's

In the summer, the Ruddy Duck male, which lives in marshes, has chestnut colored plumage and its bill is blue. In the winter, 6 therefore, the male is brown with a creamy colored face.

6
A) NO CHANGE
B) for instance,
C) on the other hand,
D) consequently,

ANSWERS AND EXPLANATIONS: PROOFREADER PROBLEM SET 1

1. **C** When **transitions** are tested, check to see whether the ideas agree or disagree with each other. Saving for retirement and throwing away money on lottery tickets are opposite ideas. Eliminate (A), (B), and (D) because they all indicate that the ideas agree. Choice (C) is the correct answer.

2. **A** The different vocabulary in the answers indicates that this question tests **precision**. *Ordinary* is the word that makes most sense in describing a *summer cottage*, so choose (A).

3. **D** This sentence contains a **verb consistency** error. The subject *she* is singular, so the verb must also be singular. Eliminate (A) and (B) because the verbs are plural. The next issue is the **verb tense.** *Has been* is the present perfect tense while *was* is the simple past tense. The perfect tense is not needed, so eliminate (C). The correct answer is (D).

4. **D** The question contains a **verb tense** issue. Although the documentary is discussed in the present tense, the subject of the underlined verb is the *political system of the 1920s*, which is in the past. Only (C) and (D) are in the past. The *system* is singular, so the correct answer is (D).

5. **C** The pronoun *their* (plural) refers to the collective noun ABBA (singular). Remember to check **pronouns** for **consistency** with the noun they replace. Watch out for (D). *It's* means *it is*.

6. **C** When checking **transitions,** determine whether it should be the same or opposite direction. The sentence describes a change from *summer* to *winter*, so the correct answer is (C). Only *on the other hand* indicates opposite ideas.

PROOFREADER PROBLEM SET 2

Visitors to the zoo have often looked into exhibits designed for **1** lions and seen ducks or crows eating treats or enjoying water intended for the large cats.

1

A) NO CHANGE

B) lions, and

C) lions; and

D) lions: and

Before the sun **2** rose yesterday, Rebecca has already awoken and begun her morning regimen of activities.

2

A) NO CHANGE

B) rose yesterday, Rebecca had already awoken and begun

C) had arisen yesterday, Rebecca has already awoken and begun

D) rose yesterday, Rebecca had already awoken and begin

Jill knows that she performs worse on multiple-choice tests than on short answer **3** tests; where she is required to show her understanding in writing.

3

A) NO CHANGE

B) tests; whereby

C) tests, also

D) tests, in which

The woman in the front row of the audience told us that the thriller was the scariest movie that **4** they had ever seen.

4

A) NO CHANGE

B) they have

C) she had

D) she have

To **5** ritualize its bicentennial, the town threw a day-long festival followed by an hour-long fireworks display.

5

A) NO CHANGE

B) celebrate

C) admire

D) greet

To be a good psychologist, one must **6** be, trustworthy, kind, and patient, or one's clients will not feel comfortable.

6

A) NO CHANGE

B) be trustworthy, kind, and,

C) be trustworthy, kind, and

D) be trustworthy kind and

ANSWERS AND EXPLANATIONS: PROOFREADER PROBLEM SET 2

1. **A**   This is about **punctuation**. Use the Vertical Line Test. The first part of the sentence, up to *lions*, is complete. The second part of the sentence, after *and*, is incomplete. No STOP punctuation is allowed. (Remember that a comma + FANBOYS is STOP.) Eliminate (B) and (C). As for (D), there is no good reason to take a pause after *lions*. NO CHANGE is necessary.

2. **B**   The verb *has already awoken* is in the present perfect **tense**, but the sentence is referring to something that happened in the past, before yesterday's sunrise. The past perfect tense, *had already awoken*, is required, and (D) is incorrect because it switches tense by using *begin* instead of *begun*.

3. **D**   Use the Vertical Line Test for **punctuation** changes. Choices (A) and (B) are incorrect, since STOP punctuation cannot be used with incomplete ideas. In (C), using the word *also* creates two complete ideas. (Note: Use the word *where* only to refer to places; in this sentence it incorrectly refers to *short answer tests*. Therefore, *in which*, as in (D), is correct.)

4. **C**   First, check **pronoun consistency.** The subject is *The woman* so the pronoun must be *she*. Eliminate (A) and (B). Next, consider **verb consistency.** Because *she* is singular, the plural verb *have* can be eliminated. Choice (C) is correct.

5. **B**   The choices contain different vocabulary, so this is a **precision** issue. The town had a *festival* and *fireworks*, so the answer needs to indicate a party. Only (B), *celebrate*, has the correct meaning.

6. **C**   This question tests **commas.** There is a list in the sentence, so look for the one that separates the items with commas. Choices (A) and (B) both have too many commas, and (D) doesn't have any. The correct answer is (C).

PROOFREADER PROBLEM SET 3

1 <u>Accept for</u> chocolate desserts in restaurants, I generally avoid eating sugar, cake, and candy in order to stay healthy.

1
A) NO CHANGE
B) Except for
C) Accepting
D) In spite of

Although pennies seem to be cheap and inconsequential donations, charities agree that **2** <u>it adds</u> up to a significant sum.

2
A) NO CHANGE
B) it does add
C) they add
D) they added

3 <u>Against the advice of its coach,</u> who has led many teams to victory, this year's baseball team attended more parties than practices and had an especially disappointing season.

3
A) NO CHANGE
B) Against the advice of their coach
C) As opposed to the advice of their coach
D) Against the advice of it's coach

The ongoing costs associated with feeding so many tigers and the difficulties caused by meddling neighbors **4** <u>has not been considered</u> prior to purchasing the land and building the animal sanctuary.

4
A) NO CHANGE
B) were not considered
C) was not considered
D) has not been in consideration

Manny's mother always has snacks on
5 hand—unlike Nick's father.

5

A) NO CHANGE

B) hand unlike

C) hand; unlike

D) hand. Unlike

The humpback **6** whale famous for
composing unique songs, that can be as long
as 20 minutes, typically migrates as far as
25,000 kilometers a year.

6

A) NO CHANGE

B) whale, famous for composing unique
songs

C) whale famous for composing unique
songs

D) whale, famous for composing unique
songs,

ANSWERS AND EXPLANATIONS: PROOFREADER PROBLEM SET 3

1. **B** Here, the author uses incorrect **diction**. The word *accept* means "to receive" something offered. The author should have chosen *except*, which means "to the exclusion of."

2. **C** This **pronoun consistency** question has the singular word *it* referring to the plural words *pennies* and *donations*. Don't choose (D); that one changes the tense.

3. **A** **Pronoun Consistency**: The *team* is singular. *Its* is its singular match. *Their* is plural. *It's* means *it is*.

4. **B** The **verb** *has not been considered* is singular, but it should stay **consistent** with the plural subject *costs...and difficulties*. Only *were* is plural in these options. Kudos if you also noticed that *prior to purchasing* means we need the past tense.

5. **A** Use the Vertical Line Test for **punctuation** changes. Choices (C) and (D) are incorrect, since STOP punctuation cannot be used with incomplete ideas. The ideas do need to be separated, so a punctuation is needed. The HALF-STOP is used correctly, so the answer is (A).

6. **B** Only the **commas** are changing, so look for a list or unnecessary information. The phrase *famous for composing unique songs that can be as long as 20 minutes* can be removed from the sentence, making it unnecessary. Therefore, it should be surrounded by commas, making the answer (B).

PROOFREADER PROBLEM SET 4

The United States and the Philippines **1** is the top choice for a mining contract.

1
A) NO CHANGE
B) are the top choice
C) is the top choices
D) are the top choices

Anyone trying a yoga pose for the first time should follow her **2** gurus instructions—otherwise, she may injure herself.

2
A) NO CHANGE
B) gurus' instruction's
C) gurus instruction's
D) guru's instructions

Though popular mainly as a device that played music, Edison's phonograph **3** is originally created as an educational tool to teach spelling and allow deaf people to hear recordings of books.

3
A) NO CHANGE
B) was
C) will be
D) have been

The parties spent many hours in meetings together with an arbiter to mediate the dispute. **4** Nevertheless, they were unable to reach an agreement.

4
A) NO CHANGE
B) Moreover,
C) Instead,
D) Consequently,

The current practice of removing endangered species from their natural habitats and placing them in zoos **5** are under debate.

5

A) NO CHANGE

B) is

C) were

D) have been

Alien species piggybacking on human travelers to new countries are wreaking havoc on planet Earth, though **6** they live for only a short time.

6

A) NO CHANGE

B) they are living

C) the alien species live

D) some of them live

ANSWERS AND EXPLANATIONS: PROOFREADER PROBLEM SET 4

1. **D** The subject is *The United States and the Philippines* and requires the plural verb *are*. Two countries are plural and thus *choices* is most **consistent**.

2. **D** When checking **apostrophes,** check for possession. The *instructions* belong to the *guru* but nothing belongs to the *instructions*. Choice (D) is correct because only *guru* needs the apostrophe.

3. **B** The changes in these answers pertain to verb **tense**. To match the past tense established and used elsewhere in the sentence (*played, created*), the past tense *was* is needed.

4. **A** Although *Nevertheless* sounds like a clumsy **transition,** there is no error in the sentence as written. Try not to eliminate answers just because they "sound bad." Choices (B) and (D) do not indicate the proper direction. *Instead* doesn't work in context. That leaves only (A).

5. **B** Although it might look like a tense issue, first check that the verb is **consistent** with its subject. The subject is the *practice* (all that other stuff, from *of removing* to *in zoos* describes the subject but is not itself the subject), so the verb must be singular. Only (B) is singular.

6. **C** The original sentence contains an **ambiguous pronoun;** it is unclear who *they* is referring to. Only (C) uses a noun to create the precise meaning.

EDITOR PROBLEM SET 1

In these days of pollution, one must clean one's car with something other than rain. There are many car washing techniques available and they each have their pluses and minuses.

1 The most annoying grime to clean off a car is bird poop. Basically it's a stream of water at a really high force like a fire hose's pressure. But not everybody likes touch-free because it might not get off really tough dirt and stains. Sometimes scrubbing is necessary.

2 For a scrubbing function, do not use a touch-free car wash. The traditional car wash with the waving strips of cloth that touch the exterior runs the risk of scratching the car, especially if the cloth strips have bits of dirt or gravel from the last car. But the strips can rub the stains out more successfully **3** for about the same amount of money.

1

Which choice provides the most effective introduction to the paragraph?

A) NO CHANGE

B) Many people prefer the touch-free car wash because it does not scratch car paint.

C) It's not worth getting the car washed in the spring because pollen will coat the car every day.

D) The cheapest way to get your car clean is to hire a kid from the neighborhood to wash it.

2

Which choice provides the best transition from the previous paragraph to this one?

A) NO CHANGE

B) Nevertheless, a touch-free car wash has other advantages.

C) Because a stream of water is never enough to cut through dirt, one should avoid a touch-free car wash.

D) For tougher dirt, one should use a car wash that physically scrubs the car.

3

The writer wants to add a supporting detail to explain the statement in the first part of this sentence. Which choice best accomplishes this goal?

A) NO CHANGE

B) and uses less water.

C) if the car is in there long enough.

D) with friction added to the standard soap and water mixture.

The best type of car wash is done by hand, though it can take a couple hours of your time. You can get all the dirt off without scratching your **4** car. However, you must be careful and thorough. **5**

Of course, **6** don't get too excited because a lot of messed-up stuff can happen. When you wash a car by hand, you might end up getting soapy or wet as you work. That makes hand washing a much better idea in the summer—if you try it in the winter, you might just freeze!

4

Which choice most effectively combines the sentences at the underlined portion?

A) car, but being careful and thorough is a necessity.

B) car if you are careful and thorough.

C) car; therefore thoroughness is required and you must be carful.

D) car, for you must be careful and thorough.

5

At this point the writer is considering adding the following sentence.

> Another benefit is that washing for hours by hand can be a good workout.

Should the writer make this addition?

A) Yes, because it supports the argument that washing by hand is the best kind of car wash.

B) Yes, because it encourages people to spend more time outside.

C) No, because it is not relevant to the comparison of efficacy among the different methods of car washing.

D) No, because it doesn't consider that some might not agree that washing a car is a form of exercise.

6

Which choice is most consistent with the writer's style and tone throughout the passage?

A) NO CHANGE

B) even the best method can have drawbacks.

C) despite the awesomeness of hand washing, it has some bummers too.

D) nothing is perfect and you're bound to be disappointed no matter what.

ANSWERS AND EXPLANATIONS: EDITOR PROBLEM SET 1

1. **B** An introductory sentence should be **consistent** with the other information in the paragraph. Only the *touch-free car wash* can be described as *a stream of water at a really high force.*

2. **D** When choosing a **transition** between paragraphs, look for a sentence that connects the ideas. This paragraph is no longer about *a touch-free car wash,* so eliminate (A), (B), and (C). Choice (D) effectively transitions from the touch-free to the scrubbing car wash.

3. **D** For a support question, the information must be **consistent** with the sentence or paragraph. Only *friction* is consistent with *cloth that touch* and *rub the stains out.*

4. **B** When combining sentences, chose the most **concise** choice that keeps the original **meaning.** The transitions *but, therefore,* and *for* change the meaning, so they're out. Choice (B) is short and consistent in meaning.

5. **C** If the sentence doesn't play a **precise** role in the argument, it should not be added. There's no debate about exercise, so eliminate (D) and choose (C).

6. **B** The tone must stay **consistent.** Choices (A), (C), and (D) are too slangy to match the tone of the passage.

EDITOR PROBLEM SET 2

Many people think that those living near an active volcano should be forced to move to a safer home. This might seem to make sense, but there are good reasons why they should be permitted to keep their homes.

[1] First of all, many people think a volcano is a dangerous place to live, **1** and they would never build their homes there in the first place. [2] Sometimes an active volcano just drizzles out lava. [3] Other places have their own potential problems. [4] Living on the coast is dangerous because of hurricanes, living in the Midwest is dangerous because of tornados, and living in low-elevation areas is dangerous because of flash flooding. [5] People should learn to **2** face their fears because there is no truly safe place to live. **3**

1

The writer wants to add a supporting detail to counter the statement in the first part of this sentence. Which choice best accomplishes this goal?

A) NO CHANGE

B) yet many volcanoes are on beautiful tropical islands.

C) so those living near volcanoes should be forced to move before something terrible happens.

D) but many of the world's active volcanoes are surrounded by cities and have remained quiet for centuries.

2

Which choice most effectively suggests that danger is something people must learn to live with?

A) NO CHANGE

B) run away from

C) look at

D) surrender to

3

To improve the cohesion and flow of this paragraph, the writer wants to add the following sentence.

> Slow, predictable lava flow is not much of a hazard.

The sentence would most logically be placed

A) after sentence 1.

B) after sentence 2.

C) after sentence 3.

D) after sentence 4.

[4] Secondly, people should be allowed to live where they choose. Perhaps those who dare to live beside a volcano do so because they have a good view or a fertile garden. Maybe they live near their families and friends. Maybe they have a house that has been in their family for generations. **[5]** Despite these realities, the government should not force them to move because of the possibility of disaster. **[6]** They have something precious that is worth sustaining all these scary possibilities for: a home.

Which choice provides the best introduction to the paragraph while maintaining the focus of the passage?

A) NO CHANGE

B) In addition, scientists have become very good at predicting when a volcano will erupt, so people will have plenty of time to evacuate.

C) Worst of all is living near a fault line, where a devastating earthquake could happen at any moment.

D) Lastly, it's more expensive to move than to rebuild.

Which choice provides the most effective transition between ideas in the paragraph?

A) NO CHANGE

B) For all these reasons,

C) Misunderstanding their excuses,

D) Against these justifications,

At this point the writer is considering adding the following sentence.

> In this country people have the right to life, liberty, and the pursuit of happiness.

Should the writer make this addition?

A) Yes, because it provides an example of why the government shouldn't tell people where to live.

B) Yes, because it highlights that people can be happy wherever they choose to live.

C) No, because it interrupts the flow of the argument.

D) No, because it counters the argument being made.

ANSWERS AND EXPLANATIONS: EDITOR PROBLEM SET 2

1. **D** The best answer must be **consistent** with the purpose stated in the question. The supporting detail must be counter to the idea that *a volcano is a dangerous place to live*. Stating that volcanos *have remained quiet for centuries* is the only counter, so choose (D). Choices (A) and (C) are similar to the first idea. Choice (B) might be a good reason to stay but doesn't counter the idea that volcanos are dangerous.

2. **A** The word must be **consistent** with the idea that *danger is something people must learn to live with*. Eliminate (B) and (D) because they mean the opposite. Choice (A) gives the most precise meaning to the sentence.

3. **B** The sentence should be placed where it is **consistent** in focus with the sentences before and after it. This new sentence relates to why people do not need to fear living near a volcano. Sentence 1 gets at that, but it's not until sentence 2 that lava is mentioned (*an active volcano just drizzles out lava*). By following that, the new sentence most explicitly makes the point that some volcanoes are not very dangerous. Sentence 3 changes topic to talk about other types of natural disasters and sentence 4 focuses on facing one's fears; neither is as connected to the topic as (B).

4. **A** A topic sentence must be **consistent** with the other information in the passage. The passage discusses why people *should be permitted to keep their homes* and this paragraph states that *the government should not force them to move*. Only (A) is consistent with those ideas.

5. **B** A transition must be **consistent** with the sentences it connects. Choices (A), (C), and (D) incorrectly indicate that this sentence will be different from the previous sentences. Therefore, (B), which contains a same-direction transition, is the correct answer.

6. **C** If the sentence doesn't play a **precise** role in the argument, it should not be added. Eliminate (A) and (B). The sentence doesn't *counter* the argument, so eliminate (D) and choose (C).

Chapter 7
Writing and Language Practice Test

Writing and Language Test

35 MINUTES, 44 QUESTIONS

Turn to Section 2 of your answer sheet to answer the questions in this section.

DIRECTIONS

Each passage below is accompanied by a number of questions. For some questions, you will consider how the passage might be revised to improve the expression of ideas. For other questions, you will consider how the passage might be edited to correct errors in sentence structure, usage, or punctuation. A passage or a question may be accompanied by one or more graphics (such as a table or graph) that you will consider as you make revising and editing decisions.

Some questions will direct you to an underlined portion of a passage. Other questions will direct you to a location in a passage or ask you to think about the passage as a whole.

After reading each passage, choose the answer to each question that most effectively improves the quality of writing in the passage or that makes the passage conform to the conventions of standard written English. Many questions include a "NO CHANGE" option. Choose that option if you think the best choice is to leave the relevant portion of the passage as it is.

Questions 1–11 are based on the following passage.

Adventures in Cooking

"Turn off the stove!" I told my sister in a panicked voice, lifting the overflowing pot of water off the hot stove. I had never cooked dinner before, and it was much more difficult than I thought it would be. Already I had burned the dinner **1** rolls dropped an egg, on the floor, and now this. To make matters worse, cooking was **2** not the first, nor the only, household chore I'd tackled with disastrous results.

1
A) NO CHANGE
B) rolls, dropped an egg, on the floor and
C) rolls, dropped an egg on the floor, and
D) rolls, dropped an egg on the floor and,

2
A) NO CHANGE
B) not even the first
C) far from being the first and only
D) not alone in its being a

CONTINUE

When I began high **3** school, my parents gave me a choice, I could cook dinner every evening after school, or I could do the laundry. I tried to do the laundry, with disastrous results. Somehow a red sock ended up in a load of white clothes, and as a result my entire family had to contend with blotchy, stained pink shirts. **4** Pink is my favorite color, so I was not too upset.

[1] After that catastrophic first dinner, **5** when I decided that I needed to learn more about cooking. [2] First, I read my grandmother's cookbooks, but the recipes directed me to do mysterious things such as "blanch" and "sauté." [3] Many ingredients were puzzling too. [4] What exactly was a "shallot" or a "scape"? [5] Clearly, I was not fluent in the cryptic language of cooking. **6**

3

A) NO CHANGE

B) school, my parents gave me a choice

C) school, my parents gave me a choice:

D) school my parents gave me a choice.

4

Which sentence provides the most logical transition between this paragraph and the next one?

A) NO CHANGE

B) Following that debacle, I was reassigned to the kitchen.

C) I decided to stop doing laundry.

D) I cannot do yard work properly, either.

5

A) NO CHANGE

B) at which

C) then

D) DELETE the underlined portion.

6

To make this paragraph most coherent, sentence 5 should be placed

A) where it is now.

B) before sentence 1.

C) before sentence 2.

D) before sentence 3.

CONTINUE

For a few weeks, my family suffered through my unsuccessful attempts at spaghetti, tacos, **7** and hamburgers. **8** "I hope you don't aspire to be a chef!" my older brother joked.

Then one evening, I began watching a television show called "Iron Chef." The show was filmed in Japan, with Japanese contestants and announcers; **9** instead, for an American audience, the voices were dubbed over in English. "Iron Chef" portrayed a contest between two skilled chefs.

10 He was given one hour to create multiple dishes, all of which had to contain the "ingredient of the day." Sometimes the designated ingredient was a common food, such as chicken. More often, however, the ingredient was something unusual, like yams, eggplant, or kiwi. Each chef was allowed to use other ingredients, but the judges' task was to determine which meal best expressed **11** certain unique qualities.

The announcers on "Iron Chef" could have been sports commentators because their remarks were enthusiastic, well-informed, and interesting. "Iron Chef" was amusing, and it taught me how to cook. Never again did I serve burned, bland pasta.

7

A) NO CHANGE
B) and I burned the
C) after that
D) and making

8

At this point, the author wants to add a sentence that supports the statement made in the previous sentence. Which choice best accomplishes this goal?

A) Hamburgers are not healthy.
B) I do not think I will attend cooking school.
C) Everything I cooked was burned and tasteless.
D) It is difficult to cook hamburgers properly, but I needed to learn.

9

A) NO CHANGE
B) moreover,
C) in fact,
D) accordingly,

10

A) NO CHANGE
B) Each was
C) Each were
D) The chef was

11

A) NO CHANGE
B) its
C) some
D) the designated ingredient's

CONTINUE

Questions 12–22 are based on the following passage.

Privy to the Past

In 2017, Boston's City Archaeologist, Joe Bagley, and his team began digging into the ground surrounding an old brick house in the North End neighborhood. Historical records indicate how the property evolved from a private home in the Revolutionary War [12] era; to an apartment complex in the nineteenth century. Although the Pierce-Hichborn house is Boston's fifth-oldest structure, the property had never been excavated by archaeologists. [13] Consequently, Bagley wasn't sure what his team would uncover. The archaeologists carefully examined shallow strips of dirt. Then they stopped: they had uncovered a small rectangular brick structure. The team was elated. "The one thing that we always want to find is a privy," Bagley explained.

Before the introduction of indoor plumbing, many houses in Boston and elsewhere [14] dumped human waste via privies, or outdoor toilets. These outhouses typically involved a foundation of stone, brick, or wood at ground level that covered a hole [15] dug downward about six feet into the earth. This appeared to be one such building.

12
A) NO CHANGE
B) era,
C) era—
D) era

13
A) NO CHANGE
B) Indeed,
C) Likewise,
D) Moreover,

14
Which choice best maintains the style and tone of the passage?
A) NO CHANGE
B) jettisoned
C) disposed of
D) chucked

15
A) NO CHANGE
B) dug
C) dug roughly
D) dug deeply; it was necessary to go

CONTINUE

Conventional archaeology has shied away from studying the contents of ancient toilets, but material uncovered in these sites **16** have provided important clues for understanding our ancestors' lives. Examining excrement from a privy can teach scientists what foods people ate, where food was prepared, and even what parasites were present in a given community.

From the time of the ancient Romans, toilets were **17** often found in public spaces, so archaeologists often find scraps of cookware, glass, and other domestic artifacts in privies. Older artifacts often appear farther underground than newer ones, but archaeologists also analyze the composition of ceramics, window shards, and **18** the makeup of pigments to determine their age and origin. Consequently, these objects can provide specific details about the status of properties and commercial goods at particular historical **19** moments, including where the local tavern was located, what kind of dishes were available for purchase, and who owned what kinds of buttons.

16

A) NO CHANGE

B) were

C) has

D) have had

17

Which choice most effectively sets up the examples named later in the sentence?

A) NO CHANGE

B) likely to feature both graffiti and vermin,

C) sometimes linked to urban sewer systems,

D) also utilized as household disposal sites,

18

A) NO CHANGE

B) pigments

C) those of pigments

D) pigments' composition

19

A) NO CHANGE

B) moments; including

C) moments, among these have been

D) moments. Including

CONTINUE

At the Pierce-Hichborn house, [20] they identified some pieces of eighteenth-century coal and the handle of a beer stein before temporarily halting their excavation of the site. When they resumed, they shifted from removing shallow, exploratory strips of ground to excavating a larger, deeper [21] area. To study how the property had transformed across generations, Bagley admitted that he hoped the toilet proved to be at least six feet deep: [22] "it was a good place to basically make your garbage disappear."

20

A) NO CHANGE

B) Bagley's team

C) he

D) Boston colonists

21

The writer is considering revising the underlined portion to the following.

> area that, as a likely privy site, promised to yield the greatest concentration of material for analysis.

Should the writer make this revision here?

A) Yes, because it provides necessary information about privies that is not available elsewhere.

B) Yes, because it clarifies why the scientists changed their method of exploration.

C) No, because it does not give enough detail about what the archaeologists hoped to find.

D) No, because it does not explain why having more material to analyze is desirable.

22

The writer wants to conclude the passage with a quotation from Bagley that explains his hopes for the privy site prior to fully excavating it. Which choice most effectively accomplishes this goal?

A) NO CHANGE

B) "most people would throw their household garbage into the outhouse because it was smelly."

C) "that gives us the best opportunity to find a lot of things from multiple families."

D) "if you want to dig, you can dig."

CONTINUE

Questions 23–33 are based on the following passage.

Esperanto: a Communications Solution?

Is world peace an unobtainable ideal? Since thousands of languages are [23] spoken aloud across the globe, communication among different populations is often strained. [24] While English is growing as an international language, its use is not without complications. Non-native [25] speakers, who often feel that they are at a linguistic or cultural disadvantage, can resent its status as a *lingua franca*.

The need for an [26] affective, and neutral means of international communication struck Dr. L. L. Zamenhof, who in the late nineteenth century [27] evolved the language Esperanto.

[23]
A) NO CHANGE
B) in verbal use
C) communicated orally
D) spoken

[24]
A) NO CHANGE
B) Nonetheless,
C) However,
D) In addition,

[25]
A) NO CHANGE
B) speakers who often feel
C) speakers, who often feel,
D) speakers who often feel,

[26]
A) NO CHANGE
B) effective and
C) affective and
D) effective, and

[27]
A) NO CHANGE
B) grew
C) executed
D) developed

CONTINUE

Zamenhof **28** has designed the language to be easily learned. Features of **29** Esperanto include: completely regular forms, simple grammar, and a rich root system. Much of the vocabulary is eerily familiar to those with some knowledge of Western European languages.

Though Esperanto is not currently widespread enough to be a realistic solution to world communication problems, it is potentially another step towards global harmony. Esperanto is the most successful constructed language to date. It is estimated that as many as two million people use Esperanto as a second language. **30** Another 100,000 people are considered native speakers because they began learning the language at birth.

There is no shortage of material in Esperanto for learners of the language to enjoy. Although many of the books published in Esperanto have been translated from other languages, there are hundreds of works in print that were first written in Esperanto. Esperanto's reach has even penetrated the world of film: *Incubus*, a 1965 movie starring William Shatner, was filmed entirely in Esperanto. **31**

28

A) NO CHANGE
B) had designed
C) designed
D) was designing

29

A) NO CHANGE
B) Esperanto include,
C) Esperanto include
D) Esperanto:

30

Which choice provides the most relevant supporting information to the paragraph?

A) NO CHANGE
B) This is impressive, considering how much of Esperanto is derived from the supposedly "dead" language of Latin.
C) It's a good bet a fair number of those speakers have heard of Zamenhof.
D) These people are in a good position to evaluate how effective Esperanto is for communicating ideas.

31

At this point, the writer is considering adding the following sentence.

> Shatner is perhaps most famous for his role as Captain Kirk in the original *Star Trek* series.

Should the writer make this addition here?

A) Yes, because it provides more information about a person who has spoken Esperanto.
B) Yes, because it reinforces the writer's point about the success of Esperanto.
C) No, because it fails to take into account the effect of Captain Kirk's fluency with languages.
D) No, because it blurs the focus of the paragraph by introducing loosely related information.

CONTINUE

Though opponents have voiced their skepticism about the language, the community of Esperantists continues to grow. **32** For most of the 20th century, Esperanto proponents relied on various means to establish an international community. These included travel, letter-writing, newsletters, and conferences that brought speakers together. In this century, the internet has fueled Esperanto's growth by providing easy access to learning platforms such as Duolingo that teach the language and apps such as Amikumu that facilitate finding other nearby speakers.

The promise of international cooperation is what keeps many Esperantists motivated. Only time will tell, however, whether Esperanto will help achieve this goal. **33**

32

Which choice most effectively combines the underlined sentences?

A) For most of the 20th century, Esperanto speakers relied on various means to establish an international community, and these means included travel, letter-writing, newsletters, and conferences.

B) For most of the 20th century, Esperanto proponents relied on means such as travel, letter-writing, newsletters, and conferences to establish an international community of speakers.

C) Travel, letter-writing, newsletters, and conferences were some of the various means upon which 20th century speakers of Esperanto relied in order to establish an international community of speakers.

D) For most of the 20th century, Esperanto proponents relied on various means, including travel, letter-writing, newsletters, and conferences among others, to establish an international community of speakers including:

33

Which choice provides a concluding sentence that most effectively refers back to ideas in the introductory paragraph?

A) With any luck it won't fail!

B) As of now, however, its prospects are dismal.

C) So grab your copy of *Incubus* and make a toast to Esperanto's creator, Dr. Zamenhof!

D) Until then, pacon! Peace!

CONTINUE

Questions 34–44 are based on the following passage.

International Politics and the Birth of the Atomic Bomb

The history of the atomic bomb is marked by strange intersections of international politics [34] yet astounding science. Marie Curie was born in Warsaw, Poland, at a time when that city was [35] under Russian occupation. She moved first to Austrian-controlled Cracow and then to Paris, where her work earned her two prizes from the Scandinavian-based Nobel Prize Committees.

[36] Nevertheless, thirty years later, in 1938, German scientists Otto Hahn and Fritz Strassman [37] discovered that they could split the nucleus of a uranium atom. This "fission," as it was named a year later, released extra neutrons that could in turn split other radioactive atoms. [38] With war looming on the horizon, some members of the worldwide scientific community began to suspect that the energy released in this chain reaction could, in theory, be harnessed to create a bomb with unprecedented power.

34

A) NO CHANGE
B) but
C) as well as
D) DELETE the underlined portion.

35

A) NO CHANGE
B) beneath
C) below
D) doomed to

36

Which choice provides the best transition from the previous paragraph to this one?

A) NO CHANGE
B) Perhaps not surprisingly, in 1938
C) The political landscape was still quite complicated in 1938 when
D) Curie had already been dead for four years when, in 1938,

37

A) NO CHANGE
B) puzzled over
C) tripped over
D) had a lucky accident to know

38

A) NO CHANGE
B) War loomed on the horizon,
C) As the war, which loomed on the horizon,
D) The war that was looming on the horizon would make

CONTINUE

Leo Szilard, the son of a Hungarian Jewish civil engineer, studied under Albert Einstein in Germany. After Hitler came to **39** power, he fled Germany for England, and there published his views on the possibility of a neutron chain reaction. **40** In anticipation of the outbreak of World War II, Szilard fled to New York City, where he became a professor at Columbia **41** University, in the same year, that Hahn and Strassman made their fateful discovery.

Szilard studied Hahn and Strassman's results and the work of other German scientists, which **42** suggested that a few pounds of uranium could have the same explosive and destructive power as many thousands of pounds of dynamite. Szilard contacted Einstein about the potential threat this posed, and in August 1939 succeeded in encouraging Einstein to write to President Franklin D. Roosevelt with a warning that Germany was attempting to develop a nuclear weapon and that the United States should preempt the threat by developing one first.

39

A) NO CHANGE
B) power he fled
C) power, Szilard fled
D) power Szilard fled,

40

At this point, the writer is considering adding the following sentence.

Szilard had left Germany in 1933 to escape Nazi persecution and continue his work in other parts of Europe.

Should the writer make this addition here?

A) Yes, because it indicates that some scientists felt compelled to leave Germany for their safety as well as to avoid lending their knowledge to the Nazi's side.

B) Yes, because it helps explain why Germany would not be pursuing nuclear weapons.

C) No, because it detracts from the flow of the passage, and where Szilard fled is not as important as the fact that he left Nazi Germany.

D) No, because Hitler did not win a majority vote and he was not able to challenge important scientists at this time.

41

A) NO CHANGE
B) University; in the same year
C) University: in the same year
D) University in the same year

42

A) NO CHANGE
B) would suggest
C) could have suggested
D) suggests

CONTINUE ►

In September 1941, two of the most knowledgeable atomic scientists met to discuss the recent attempts of making the theory of atomic power a militaristic reality **43** at a meeting in Nazi-occupied Copenhagen, Denmark. German physicist Werner Heisenberg, who had continued his work in Nazi Germany, sought out his former mentor, the Danish scientist Nils Bohr. Bohr had pioneered atomic theories but his work had been impeded by the persecution of the Nazi forces occupying his country. Although it was supposed to be secret, the meeting was almost certainly compromised due to the wartime surveillance Bohr endured, and thus, the men were exceedingly nervous. Unable to speak freely, Heisenberg talked in an indirect manner. Heisenberg spoke so vaguely because he feared charges of treason for giving up German secrets.

In 1943, Bohr made the momentous choice to refuse to work on the German atomic bomb, and he fled to Sweden, then to London, and eventually ended up in the United States.

43

A) NO CHANGE

B) while attending a meeting

C) while in attendance at a meeting

D) attending a meeting

This decision may have determined the course of the war. The most world-renowned physicists were gathered in the U.S. to work on the Manhattan Project, **44** a project that has cost U.S. taxpayers more than any other in history. These esteemed scientists considered Bohr the sage of the group: The side that had Bohr was the side that would have the bomb.

44

Which choice most accurately and effectively represents the information in the graph?

A) NO CHANGE

B) a project that cost more to administer than even the Apollo space program.

C) a project that costs far less than comparable energy programs.

D) a project that received annual funding from 1942 to 1946.

Annual Funding for Manhattan Project, Apollo Program, and DOE Energy Technology R&D Program

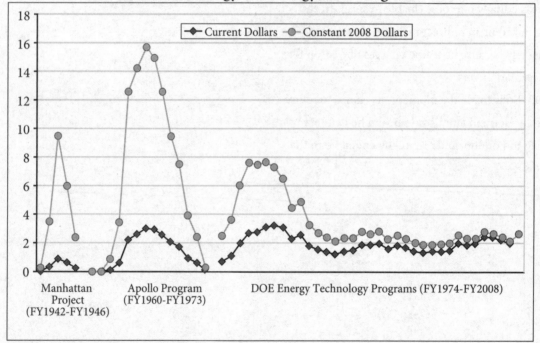

Chapter 8
Writing and
Language Practice
Test: Answers and
Explanations

WRITING AND LANGUAGE TEST ANSWER KEY

1.	C		23.	D
2.	B		24.	A
3.	C		25.	A
4.	B		26.	B
5.	D		27.	D
6.	A		28.	C
7.	A		29.	C
8.	C		30.	A
9.	D		31.	D
10.	B		32.	B
11.	D		33.	D
12.	D		34.	C
13.	A		35.	A
14.	C		36.	C
15.	B		37.	A
16.	C		38.	A
17.	D		39.	C
18.	B		40.	C
19.	A		41.	D
20.	B		42.	A
21.	B		43.	B
22.	C		44.	D

WRITING AND LANGUAGE TEST EXPLANATIONS

1. **C** The placement of the commas is changing in the answer choices, so the question is testing comma rules. The underlined portion is part of a list, so the rule here is that there should be a comma after every item in the list. The first item is *burned the dinner rolls,* which should then be followed by a comma. Eliminate (A). The second item is *dropped an egg on the floor,* which should be followed by a comma. Eliminate (B) and (D). Choice (C) is the correct answer.

2. **B** The entire phrase is changing in the answer choices, so select the most concise answer that keeps the meaning clear. If cooking was *not the first,* then there were clearly others, so the phrase *nor the only* is redundant. Eliminate (A). Eliminate (C) because *and only* is also redundant. Eliminate (D) because it uses the awkward *being* construction. Choice (B) is the correct answer.

3. **C** The first change in the answer choices is the presence of the comma after *school,* which means comma rules are being tested. Because *When I began high school* is an introductory idea, it needs to be followed by a comma. Eliminate (D). The next change in the answers is the punctuation after *choice. When I began high school, my parents gave me a choice* is a complete idea, and the second piece, *I could cook dinner every evening after school, or I could do the laundry* is also complete. Because complete ideas need to be separated by a period or its equivalent, eliminate (A) and (B). Therefore, (C) is the correct answer.

4. **B** The question asks for the transition between the paragraphs, so look for a choice that connects the ideas. Paragraph 2 starts with the choice between cooking and laundry, and it ends with an anecdote about the narrator's experience doing laundry. Paragraph 3 starts with information about the narrator's experience cooking. Both (A) and (C) don't mention *cooking,* so they relate only to paragraph 2. Eliminate (A) and (C). *Yard work* is not mentioned in either paragraph, so eliminate (D). The *debacle* refers to the laundry and the *kitchen* refers to the cooking, so (B) connects the ideas in the paragraphs. Choice (B) is the correct answer.

5. **D** One of the answer choices is to delete the underlined portion, so this question is testing concision. Consider (D) first. When the underlined portion is deleted, the phrase before the comma is an incomplete idea and the phrase after the comma is a complete idea. The comma correctly connects these parts, and the meaning of the sentence is correct. Choice (D) is the correct answer.

6. **A** The question asks where to place sentence 5, so it's testing consistency. Start by reading sentence 5, which mentions the *cryptic language of cooking.* Read the other sentences and notice that an earlier sentence mention *mysterious things,* such as *shallot* and *scrape.* The word *Clearly* in sentence 5 indicates that it should be placed after all those ideas, so it should be last in the paragraph. Choice (A) is the correct answer.

7. **A** The wording of the last item in a list is changing in the answer choices, so the question is testing consistency. In order to make the list consistent, the last item should be a noun. Choices (B), (C), and (D) are not consistent with the previous two items in the list: *spaghetti* and *tacos.* Choice (A) is the correct answer.

8. **C** The question asks for support for the previous sentence, so select the idea that's consistent. The previous sentence says that the *family suffered through my unsuccessful attempts,* so the new sentence must support that idea. *Not healthy* and *cooking school* don't relate to *unsuccessful,* so eliminate (A) and (B). The phrase *burned and tasteless* is consistent, so keep (C). Choice (D) is close, but it is too specific to the hamburgers and doesn't include the other weeks' worth of foods, so eliminate it. Choice (C) is the correct answer.

9. **D** The transitions are changing in the choices, so determine how the ideas before and after it connect. The first part says that it was *filmed in Japan,* and the second part says that the *voices were dubbed* for the American audience. The second is a natural result of the first. Eliminate (A) and (C) because they indicate a shift in direction. *Moreover* indicates more of the same, so eliminate (C). *Accordingly* correctly links the ideas. Choice (D) is the correct answer.

10. **B** The subject and the verb are changing in the answer choices, so the question is testing subject verb agreement and precision. Choice (A) uses the pronoun *he* when there are two chefs, so the use of the pronoun is not precise. Eliminate (A). Choice (D) can be eliminated for the same reason: *the chef* refers to only one of the two chefs. Both (B) and (C) use the subject *each,* which is singular, but only (B) keeps the verb consistent with the subject. Choice (B) is the correct answer.

11. **D** The choices contain both nouns and pronouns, so the question is testing clarity. The underlined portion must refer specifically to the *ingredient of the day.* Eliminate (A), (B), and (C) because they are too vague and unclear. Choice (D) is the correct answer.

12. **D** There is STOP punctuation in (A), so use the Vertical Line Test. The first part of the sentence is an incomplete idea, and the second part is also incomplete. Neither STOP nor HALF-STOP punctuation can be used after an incomplete idea, so eliminate (A) and (C). There is no need to put a comma in the sentence, so (D) is the correct answer.

13. **A** The transitions are changing, so determine how the ideas are connected. The previous sentence says that *the property had never been excavated.* This sentence says that *Bagley wasn't sure what his team would uncover.* This sentence is a result, or consequence, of the previous sentence, so (A) is the best answer.

14. **C** The tone of the passage is semi-formal. Choices (A) and (D) are too informal. Choice (B) doesn't have the correct meaning. Choice (C) is most consistent in style, tone, and meaning.

15. **B** The question is testing concision. The sentence already says *about* six feet, so *roughly* is redundant; eliminate (C). The sentence already contains the phrase *into the earth,* so *downward* is redundant; eliminate (A). Choice (D) is unnecessarily wordy. Choice (B) is the most concise, so select (B).

16. **C** The verb must be consistent in number with its subject. The subject of the verb is *material,* which is singular. Choices (A), (B) and (D) are plural, so eliminate them. Only (C) is singular.

17. **D** The examples later in the sentence are *cookware, glass, and other domestic artifacts,* so the underlined portion must be consistent with those things. Only *household disposal sites* is consistent, so the correct answer is (D).

18. **B** The sentence contains a list, so the underlined portion must be consistent with the other items in the list. The other items are *ceramics* and *window shards.* The most concise and consistent way to continue the list is *pigments,* so the correct answer is (B).

19. **A** STOP punctuation appears in some answers, so use the Vertical Line Test. The first phrase is a complete idea. For (A), (B) and (D), the second phrase is an incomplete idea. Therefore, STOP punctuation cannot be used; eliminate (B) and (D). In (C), the second phrase is a complete idea, so STOP punctuation is needed. The comma is GO punctuation, so eliminate (C). Only (A) remains.

20. **B** The pronouns "they" and "he" are unclear, so eliminate (A) and (C). It was the archeologists, not the colonists, who identified the pieces, so the answer is (B).

21. **B** The new information is consistent with the rest of the sentence and explains why the archeologists shifted their plans. Eliminate (C) and (D). It's not important information *about privies,* so eliminate (A). The best answer is (B).

22. **C** The question asks for the choices that gives Bagley's hopes for the site. Choices (A) and (B) give information about what people did in the past, but not what Bagley hopes for the site. Choice (D) is not consistent with the tone or idea of the passage. Only (C) explains what Bagley hopes to find in the site.

23. **D** The primary change in the answer choices is the inclusion of extra words, so this question is testing concision. The meaning in each answer choice is consistent with the intended meaning of the sentence. However, *spoken aloud* is redundant because speaking is implicitly something done aloud, so eliminate (A). From the remaining choices, (D) is the most concise. Therefore, (D) is the correct answer.

24. **A** Notice the transition word and the comma changing in the answer choices. The question is testing the use of transition words and commas. If a comma is used, the transition word is an introductory idea that should be followed by a complete idea, which is not consistent with the sentence that follows. Eliminate (B), (C), and (D) because they include commas. Choice (A) is the correct answer.

25. **A** The comma placement is changing in the answer choices, so the question is testing comma rules. The clause *who often feel that they are at a linguistic or cultural disadvantage* is an extra detail that is not necessary for the overall meaning of the sentence, so it should be offset with commas both before and after. Eliminate (B) and (D) because there's no comma before *who.* The comma after *feel* separates two parts of the same clause, so it cannot be included. Eliminate (C). Choice (A) is the correct answer.

26. **B**   The word *affective* is changing in the answer choices, so the question is testing the difference between *affective* and *effective*. The word *effective* is used to describe an object or action that successfully produces a desired effect while the word *affective* is related to moods and emotions. The former is the meaning that is consistent with the sentence here, so eliminate (A) and (C) because they use *affective*. The next change is the inclusion of a comma. Because you cannot use a comma with *and* in this instance, eliminate (D). Choice (B) is the correct answer.

27. **D**   The vocabulary is changing in the choices, so select the choice whose definition is consistent with the idea in the sentence. The sentence means to say that he "invented" or "created" the language Esperanto. Eliminate (A), which means "change over time." Eliminate (B), which means "to get larger." Eliminate (C), which means "to kill" or "to begin a process." *Developed* means "created." Choice (D) is the correct answer.

28. **C**   Notice the verb tense changing in the answer choices. To stay consistent with the information in the previous sentence, use simple past tense. Choice (C) is the correct answer.

29. **C**   Notice the punctuation changing after the word *include*. Choices (A) and (D) use a colon, which must follow a complete idea. Because that's not the case here, eliminate (A) and (D). Choice (B) includes a comma before a list, but commas should come between every item in a list, not before the list. Eliminate (B). Choice (C) is the correct answer.

30. **A**   The question asks for the most relevant supporting information, so select the choice that is consistent with the information in the paragraph. The paragraph says that *Esperanto is the most successful constructed language* and then supports that with the number of speakers. Choice (A) also supports that with the number of native speakers. Neither *Latin* nor *Zamenhof* adds support, so eliminate (B) and (C). Choice (D) might seem good, but it doesn't connect to the *learners* in the next sentence, so eliminate (D). Choice (A) is the correct answer.

31. **D**   The question asks whether the sentence should be added, so it's testing consistency. The paragraph is about *Esperanto* and the new sentence is about *Star Trek*. It's not consistent, so the sentence should not be added. Eliminate (A) and (B). *Kirk* is not relevant at all, so eliminate (C). Choice (D) is the correct answer.

32. **B**   The question asks for the best combination of the sentences, so it's testing concision and consistency. Start with the shortest answer choice. Choice (B) correctly connects the ideas, keeps the meaning clear, and is the shortest. Choice (B) is the correct answer.

33. **D**   The question asks for a sentence that refers to the introductory paragraph, so it's testing consistency. The introductory paragraph asks the question *Is world peace an unobtainable goal?* Only (D) refers to the idea of *peace*. Choice (D) is the correct answer.

34. **C**   The conjunction is changing in the answer choices, so the question is testing the use of conjunctions. The words *yet* and *but* are used with items in contrast, which is not consistent with the meaning of the sentence. Eliminate (A) and (B). Because the conjunction is necessary, you cannot delete the underlined portion. Eliminate (D). Choice (C) is the correct answer.

35. **A** The wording is changing in the answer choices, so the question is testing word choice. While *under*, *beneath*, and *below* can have similar meanings, the word choice must be consistent with the word that follows, *occupation*. Choices (B) and (C) do not meet this requirement. Eliminate (B) and (C). The use of the phrase *doomed to Russian occupation* would be in reference to future events, which is also not consistent with the meaning of the sentence. Choice (A) is the correct answer.

36. **C** The question asks for the best transition, so it's testing consistency. The first paragraph focuses on the *strange intersections of international politics*. Only (C) continues the idea of the *strange intersections*. Choice (C) is the correct answer.

37. **A** Notice the wording changes in the answer choices. Because the sentence discusses the scientists learning something new, (B) and (C) are not consistent with the intended meaning of the sentence. Eliminate those choices. In (D), the word *accident* changes the meaning and is not consistent with the intended meaning of the sentence. Eliminate (D). Choice (A) is the correct answer.

38. **A** Notice the wording and comma placement changing in the answer choices. The question is testing concision and punctuation. In (B) there are two complete ideas separated by a comma. Since STOP punctuation is required to separate two complete ideas, eliminate (B). Choice (C) results in an incomplete sentence, so eliminate it. Choice (D) uses the verb *would make,* which is not consistent with the verb *began* later in the sentence. Eliminate (D). Choice (A) is the correct answer.

39. **C** The first change in the answer choices is the deletion of a comma, so comma rules are being tested. *After Hitler came to power* is an introductory idea that must be followed by a comma. Eliminate (B) and (D). The next change is the use of the pronoun *he* or the name *Szilard*. The name *Szilard* is more precise than *he*, which could refer to either Szilard or Hitler. Eliminate (A). Choice (C) is the correct answer.

40. **C** The question is asking if the addition of information about where Szilard fled would benefit the passage. Because the previous sentence already mentions Szilard leaving Germany, this information is not necessary. Eliminate (A) and (B). Choice (D), which has nothing to do with the text in question, and can also be eliminated. Choice (C) is therefore the correct answer.

41. **D** The punctuation is changing in the choices, so the question is testing STOP and GO punctuation. Draw the vertical line between *University* and *in*. The first part is a complete idea, and the second part is an incomplete idea. STOP punctuation cannot be used, so eliminate (B). Eliminate (A) because there's no reason to use the comma after *year*. The phrase *he became...discovery* is one continuous thought, so there should not be any punctuation breaking up the idea. Eliminate (C). Choice (D) is the correct answer.

42. **A** The verb tense is changing in the answer choices so the question is testing verb tense rules. In order to remain consistent with the rest of the passage, use past tense. Eliminate (B), (C), and (D). Choice (A) is the correct answer.

43. **B** Notice the wording changing in the answer choices in regard to the scientists attending the meeting. Choice (A) sounds like the theories about making atomic power a militaristic reality are occurring at a particular meeting, and (D) sounds like a militaristic reality is attending a meeting. These misplaced modifiers should be eliminated. The addition of the word *while* clarifies that the scientists are the ones attending the meeting. While (B) and (C) are similar in meaning, (B) is more concise. Therefore, (B) is the correct answer.

44. **D** The question is asking for the statement that most accurately represents the information in the graph. Choices (A) and (B) state that the Manhattan Project was the most expensive project in history, but the graph indicates that the Apollo project was more expensive. Choice (C) says the Manhattan Project cost less than comparable energy programs, but this does not reflect information in the graph. Therefore, (D) is the correct answer.

Chapter 9
The Essay

THE SAT ESSAY: WHAT YOU NEED TO KNOW

The SAT includes an optional rhetorical analysis essay. Your job is to read a text (typically a speech or editorial of some sort) and discuss how the author effectively builds an argument. This might be a familiar task if you've done it in school. If not, don't worry. The format is straightforward, and with some practice, you can learn how to write a good SAT essay. In this chapter, you'll look at the three tasks you'll need to complete for the essay—reading, analysis, and writing—and you'll learn how to approach each task in the most effective way possible.

THE "OPTIONAL" ESSAY

The Essay used to be a required part of the SAT Writing test, counting for about a third of the Writing score. Some colleges found the writing score to be helpful, while others did not, so when the College Board rolled out the new SAT, they made the Essay "optional." The Essay score is now completely separate from your total score, so the essay has no effect on your 200–800 score. Notice how we're using quotation marks whenever we say the Essay is "optional," though? There's a reason for that: you should consider the Essay to be optional for colleges, but *not* optional for you.

That's because some schools require the Essay and others don't, and you can't take the Essay independently of the rest of the SAT. In other words, if you opt out of the Essay and later you realize you need it for your application, you must retake the entire SAT. So go ahead and write the Essay. You've already killed a Saturday morning and you're sitting in the testing room. Just write it. Also, as we'll show you in this chapter, it's not so ridiculously challenging to prepare for the Essay that you'll gain a lot of time from skipping it.

In short, the Essay can make your college application look more attractive. This score appears on every report you send to colleges. So regardless of whether the schools you apply to look at your essay, they'll at least see that you took the initiative to write the Essay, which is a good thing.

YOUR ESSAY MISSION

The SAT provides you with 50 minutes in which to read a text and write a logical, well-constructed analysis of that text's argument. The thing to remember here is that the College Board is **not asking you for your opinion on a topic or a text**. Your essay will be an **objective** analysis of a speech or argument.

Although the source material changes from test to test, the prompt tends to look something like this:

As you read the passage below, consider how the author uses

- evidence, such as facts or examples, to support claims.
- reasoning to develop ideas and to connect claims and evidence.
- stylistic or persuasive elements, such as word choice or appeals to emotion, to add power to the ideas expressed.

Write an essay in which you explain how [the author] builds an argument to persuade [his/her] audience that [author's claim]. In your essay, analyze how [the author] uses one or more of the features listed above (or features of your own choice) to strengthen the logic and persuasiveness of [his/her] argument. Be sure that your analysis focuses on the most relevant aspects of the passage.

Your essay should not explain whether you agree with [the author's] claims, but rather explain how the author builds an argument to persuade [his/her] audience.

In the Essay section, you will have to

- carefully read a text.
- understand how an author appeals to a reader's logic, emotions, or morals.
- write a logical analysis of an argument.
- explain how style choices can affect an author's persuasiveness.

In the Essay, you will NOT need to

- give your opinion about a text.
- memorize examples from history or literature.
- have previous experience with the text.

Two graders will read and score the essay on a 1–4 scale in three different categories: Reading, Analysis, and Writing.

> 4 = Advanced
>
> 3 = Proficient
>
> 2 = Partial
>
> 1 = Inadequate

Essay Scoring

Each category will receive a total score of 2–8, which is attained by adding the individual 1–4 scores from your two graders.) Each task (Reading, Analysis, and Writing) is scored individually, so a high score in one does *not* guarantee a high score in another. Your final Essay score will be displayed as *x/y/z*, in order, for the Reading, Analysis, and Writing domains.

TASK 1: READING

In order to write an essay that analyzes a source text, you must first read the text. Unlike with the Reading passages, there are no tricks to shorten your reading time or cut out pieces of the text. However, knowing what to look for as you read can help streamline the reading process and give you a good start on the second task of analysis.

According to the College Board, your Reading score will be based on your

- comprehension of the source text.
- understanding of central ideas, important details, and their relationship.
- accuracy in representation of the source text (i.e., no errors of fact or interpretation introduced).
- use of textual evidence (quotations, paraphrases, or both) to demonstrate understanding of the source text.

When you start the Essay task, the very first thing you have to do is read the text. Obvious, right? But reading for the Essay is more than just pleasure reading, where all you need to worry about is, say, whether Katniss is going to make it. As you read your Essay prompt, you need to consider the central idea (SOAPS) and important details that support that idea (types of appeals and style elements).

SOAPS—Like in the Tub?

SOAPS is an acronym to help you remember the five things you need to look for in order to establish the central idea of a passage or argument.

> **S**peaker
> **O**ccasion
> **A**udience
> **P**urpose
> **S**ubject

Speaker: Who is speaking or writing?

Knowing whose voice you are reading is a very important part of understanding the text. It will help you understand the author's motivations as well as the reason he or she is speaking or writing in the first place.

Occasion: What happened that requires this speech or text?

The event that caused the author to want to express his or her thoughts is an integral part of analyzing the work. It might be as simple as the type of event in which the speech was given or it could be something larger such as a significant time in a war. You will need to think about the historical context of the text.

For instance, at a wedding, a minister is likely to be optimistic and cheerful; at a funeral, a minister is more likely to be solemn and comforting. The occasion makes all the difference. Taking note of the occasion will help you understand why the author uses a certain tone and what motivates it.

Audience: Who is the intended audience?

Considering your audience is critical when you are writing a speech. Therefore, it is critical that you consider who the author's audience is in order to understand the text. What do you know about him or her? What's the relationship between the speaker/author and the intended audience? What sort of values or prior ideas might the audience have? How might that affect their perception of the speaker/author?

For example, a principal is more likely to be more informal in tone with experienced teachers and provide less detailed information than with new teachers, with whom it's important to make a good impression and establish a position of supportive authority. With new teachers, the principal will need to give clear information and perhaps repeat that information while filling them in on things that didn't need to be said to the more experienced group.

Audience can entirely change a work! When reading your source text for the essay, make sure to consider who the audience is and how that affected the way in which the author built his or her argument.

Qualifications
You should always consider what makes a person credible as an author; for instance, an avid vegetarian might have some bias in writing about the five foods you should never eat. However, on the SAT, you will never read something from an unqualified author.

Purpose: What is the author's or speaker's intention?

Occasion, Subject, and Audience all contribute to Purpose. What is the author trying to accomplish with this work? Is it an attack? Defense? Persuasion? Does it aim to give praise or blame? Is its goal to teach or is it something else?

Subject: What is the main idea?

Of course, you need to know what the work is about. What is the topic? What is the author's main point? What are the main lines of reasoning used?

Appeals

A rhetorical appeal is a persuasive strategy that authors and speakers use to support their claims (or, in a debate, to respond to opposing arguments). When a speaker or author wants to convince an audience of something, there are three main types of rhetorical appeals that can be used.

Appeal to Credibility: "Why Should I Believe You?"

This is the author's way of establishing trust with the audience. We tend to believe people whom we respect, and a good writer knows this! One of the central tasks of persuasion is to project an impression to the reader that the author is someone worth listening to, as well as someone who is likable and worthy of respect. Remember in SOAPS when we talked about the credibility of the speaker? This is how an author might use that to his or her benefit.

Appeal to Emotion: "Gee, That Made Me Feel All Warm and Fuzzy"

This is when the author tries to appeal to the reader's emotions. This allows an author or speaker to connect with an audience by using fear, humor, happiness, disgust, and so on. Imagery and language choice are often big components of appeals to emotions.

Appeal to Logic: "Well, This Just Makes Sense!"

This connects with an audience's reason or logic. This isn't logic like the formal logic in math, philosophy, or even computer science; it is the consistency and clarity of an argument as well as the logic of evidence and reasons.

> Once you find all the SOAPS points and examples of appeals, you've got what you need for the Reading task. Remember, for the Reading task, the College Board wants to see that you understand the text, can identify the central idea/theme of the text, and know how details and examples support that central idea.

TASK 2: ANALYSIS

Remember: a good score on one task does not guarantee a good score on another. Doing a good job explaining the main idea of the speech and the details that support that main idea will get you a good Reading score, but now we need to talk about the Analysis Task.

For the Analysis task, you'll have to determine the pieces of evidence, stylistic elements, or logical reasoning the author uses to effectively achieve his or her objective.

According to the College Board, your Analysis score will be based on your ability to

- analyze the source text and understand the analytical task.
- evaluate the author's use of evidence, reasoning, and/or stylistic and persuasive elements, and/or features chosen by the student.
- support claims or points made in the response.
- focus on features of the text most relevant to addressing the task.

For the second task, you will need to explain the author's use of specific elements in the essay. It's not enough to say, "The author uses a quote to appeal to the audience's reason." You have to explain *how* the quote appeals to the audience's reason. This task is all about the *how* and *why*. Look for facts, evidence, literary devices, persuasive elements, and other elements the author has used to form his or her argument.

Here are some common style elements that may show up in the text.

Style Detail	Definition	Example
Allusion	A brief reference to a person, thing, or idea from history, literature, politics, or something with cultural significance	"Don't ask him for a donation; he's a total Scrooge." "Chocolate was her Kryptonite."
Comparisons	Comparing two distinct things; the author/speaker makes a connection between them	"Juliet is the sun." "My love is like a red rose."
Diction	The author's choice of words	"Skinny" instead of "slender" sounds less flattering. Slang or vernacular gives a text an informal feel, while a professional vocabulary makes a text feel more formal.
Hyperbole	Exaggeration not meant to be taken literally	"I'm so hungry I could eat a horse."
Imagery	Using language that appeals to the senses. Visual representation of an object or idea is a common perception of imagery, but imagery actually can create ideas that appeal to all five senses.	"The woman walked by, trailing a thick, cloying cloud of perfume." "The percussive thump of the large drums vibrated in her chest as the band marched by."
Juxtaposition	Placing two ideas side-by-side in order for the audience to make a comparison or contrast	"It was the best of times, it was the worst of times…."
Repetition	Deliberate repetition of a letter, word, or phrase to achieve a specific effect.	"<u>We shall</u> not flag or fail. <u>We shall</u> go on to the end. <u>We shall</u> fight in France, <u>we shall fight</u> on the seas and oceans, <u>we shall</u> fight with growing confidence and growing strength in the air…."
Statistics or quotes	A writer or speaker may add credibility to his or her argument by adding data or quotes from a respected/recognized source.	A quote from the American Academy of Pediatrics in a speech about best practices for carseat use
Syntax	How words are put together to achieve a certain effect. First and last words of an idea can be particularly important.	An author who wants to convey a message quickly or urgently might choose to use short, direct sentences, while an author who wants to deliberately slow down a text may use longer, more convoluted sentences.
Tone	The attitude of the author/speaker toward the subject	Sarcastic, professional, critical

Note: These devices are deliberately used by the author/speaker for a specific purpose. You will need to know the purposes of the devices and their effects on a text, but you will not need to know the specific names.

Spot the Element

Read the following pieces of text and then identify the rhetorical device used in each.

1. "In our kitchen, he would bolt his orange juice (squeezed on one of those ribbed glass sombreros and then poured off through a strainer) and grab a bite of toast (the toaster a simple tin box, a kind of little hut with slit and slanted sides, that rested over a gas burner and browned one side of the bread, in stripes, at a time), and then he would dash, so hurriedly that his necktie flew back over his shoulder, down through our yard, past the grapevines hung with buzzing Japanese-beetle traps, to the yellow brick building, with its tall smokestack and wide playing fields, where he taught."

    —John Updike, "My Father on the Verge of Disgrace"

    Rhetorical device: _____

2. "Five score years ago, a great American, in whose symbolic shadow we stand today, signed the Emancipation Proclamation. This momentous decree came as a great beacon light of hope to millions of Negro slaves who had been seared in the flames of withering injustice. It came as a joyous daybreak to end the long night of their captivity."

    —Martin Luther King, Jr., "I Have a Dream"

    Rhetorical device: _____

3. "When he lifted me up in his arms I felt I had left all my troubles on the floor beneath me like gigantic concrete shoes."

    —Anne Tyler, *Earthly Possessions*

    Rhetorical device: _____

4. "Well now, one winter it was so cold that all the geese flew backward and all the fish moved south and even the snow turned blue. Late at night, it got so frigid that all spoken words froze solid afore they could be heard. People had to wait until sunup to find out what folks were talking about the night before."

    — James MacGillivray, "Paul Bunyan and Babe the Blue Ox"

    Rhetorical device: _____

5. "I was not born in a manger. I was actually born on Krypton and sent here by my father, Jor-el, to save the Planet Earth."

    —Senator Barack Obama, speech at a fund-raiser for
    Catholic charities, October 16, 2008

    Rhetorical device: _____

Answer Key

1. Imagery (visual)
2. Metaphor (beacon of light)
3. Simile
4. Hyperbole
5. Allusion

SOAPS AND APPEALS DRILL 1

See if you can identify the SOAPS and rhetorical devices used in the following prompts.

(John F. Kennedy. September 12, 1962. Rice Stadium, Houston, TX)

1   We set sail on this new sea because there is new knowledge to be gained, and new rights to be won, and they must be won and used for the progress of all people. For space science, like nuclear science and all technology, has no conscience of its own. Whether it will become a force for good or ill depends on man, and only if the United States occupies a position of pre-eminence can we help decide whether this new ocean will be a sea of peace or a new terrifying theater of war. I do not say that we should or will go unprotected against the hostile misuse of space any more than we go unprotected against the hostile use of land or sea, but I do say that space can be explored and mastered without feeding the fires of war, without repeating the mistakes that man has made in extending his writ around this globe of ours.

2   There is no strife, no prejudice, no national conflict in outer space as yet. Its hazards are hostile to us all. Its conquest deserves the best of all mankind, and its opportunity for peaceful cooperation many never come again. But why, some say, the moon? Why choose this as our goal? And they may well ask why climb the highest mountain? Why, 35 years ago, fly the Atlantic? Why does Rice play Texas?

3   We choose to go to the moon. We choose to go to the moon in this decade and do the other things, not because they are easy, but because they are hard, because that goal will serve to organize and measure the best of our energies and skills, because that challenge is one that we are willing to accept, one we are unwilling to postpone, and one which we intend to win, and the others, too.

4   It is for these reasons that I regard the decision last year to shift our efforts in space from low to high gear as among the most important decisions that will be made during my incumbency in the office of the Presidency…

5   To be sure, we are behind, and will be behind for some time in manned flight. But we do not intend to stay behind, and in this decade, we shall make up and move ahead.

6   The growth of our science and education will be enriched by new knowledge of our universe and environment, by new techniques of learning and mapping and observation, by new tools and computers for industry, medicine, the home as well as the school. Technical institutions, such as Rice, will reap the harvest of these gains.

7   And finally, the space effort itself, while still in its infancy, has already created a great number of new companies, and tens of thousands of new jobs. Space and related industries are generating new demands in investment and skilled personnel, and this city and this State, and this region, will share greatly in this growth. What was once the furthest outpost on the old frontier of the West will be the furthest outpost on the new frontier of science and

space. Houston, your City of Houston, with its Manned Spacecraft Center, will become the heart of a large scientific and engineering community. During the next 5 years the National Aeronautics and Space Administration expects to double the number of scientists and engineers in this area, to increase its outlays for salaries and expenses to $60 million a year; to invest some $200 million in plant and laboratory facilities; and to direct or contract for new space efforts over $1 billion from this Center in this City...

8   Many years ago the great British explorer George Mallory, who was to die on Mount Everest, was asked why did he want to climb it. He said, "Because it is there."

9   Well, space is there, and we're going to climb it, and the moon and the planets are there, and new hopes for knowledge and peace are there. And, therefore, as we set sail we ask God's blessing on the most hazardous and dangerous and greatest adventure on which man has ever embarked.

Thank you.

S: President John F. Kennedy

O: speaking in favor of expanded space travel

A: Rice University and Houston, Texas

P: to persuade the audience to be enthusiastic about space travel

S: difficult goals are still worth pursuing

(John F. Kennedy. September 12, 1962. Rice Stadium, Houston, TX)	***Appeal to Authority:*** *He's the President!* ***Audience:*** *Rice students, faculty, Houston residents*
We set sail on this new sea because there is new knowledge to be gained, and new rights to be won, and they must be won and used for the progress of all people.	***Purpose***
Why does Rice play Texas?	***Audience/Allusion:*** *Rice has an athletic rivalry with the University of Texas. Kennedy is showing that some challenges are inspiring.*
We choose to go to the moon. We choose to go to the moon in this decade and do the other things, not because they are easy, but because they are hard, because that goal will serve to organize and measure the best of our energies and skills, because that challenge is one that we are willing to accept, one we are unwilling to postpone, and one which we intend to win, and the others, too.	***Subject***
I regard the decision to shift our efforts in space from low to high gear as among the most important decisions made during my incumbency in the office of the Presidency…	***Occasion*** ***Appeal to Authority***
And finally, the space effort itself, while still in its infancy, has already created a great number of new companies, and tens of thousands of new jobs. Space and related industries are generating new demands in investment and skilled personnel, and this city and this State, and this region, will share greatly in this growth. What was once the furthest outpost on the old frontier of the West will be the furthest outpost on the new frontier of science and space. Houston, your City of Houston, with its Manned Spacecraft Center, will become the heart of a large scientific and engineering community. During the next 5 years the National Aeronautics and Space Administration expects to double the number of scientists and engineers in this area, to increase its outlays for salaries and expenses to $60 million a year; to invest some $200 million in plant and laboratory facilities; and to direct or contract for new space efforts over $1 billion from this Center in this City…	***Appeal to Logic/Audience:*** *Here, Kennedy is presenting the rational reasons to support the space industry: it creates jobs. We know that the audience values education and the furthering of science because JFK discusses the benefit to the scientific community as well as the medical community.*
ask God's blessing	***Audience:*** *many Texans in the 1960s would be religious people who would appreciate this reference.*

SOAPS AND APPEALS DRILL 2

Read the following prompt and underline anything that references SOAPS points. Look for rhetorical devices.

Excerpt(s) from THE RAREST OF THE RARE: VANISHING ANIMALS, TIMELESS WORLDS by Diane Ackerman, 1995. Used by permission of Random House, an imprint and division of Penguin Random House LLC. All rights reserved.

1   Leafing idly through *The Home Planet*, I stop at a picture of Earth floating against the black velvet of space. Africa and Europe are visible under swirling white clouds, but the predominant color is blue. This was the one picture from the *Apollo* missions that told the whole story—how small the planet is in the vast sprawl of space, how fragile its environments are. Seen from space, Earth has no national borders, no military zones, no visible fences. Quite the opposite. You can see how storm systems swirling above a continent may well affect the grain yield half a world away. The entire atmosphere of the planet— all the air we breathe, all the sky we fly through, even the ozone layer—is visible as the thinnest rind. The picture eloquently reminds us that Earth is a single organism. For me, the book contains visual mnemonics of how I feel about nature. At some point, one asks, "Toward what end is my life lived?" A great freedom comes from being able to answer that question. A sleeper can be decoyed out of bed by the sheer beauty of dawn on the open seas. Part of my job, as I see it, is to allow that to happen. Sleepers like me need at some point to rise and take their turn on morning watch, for the sake of the planet, but also for their own sake, for the enrichment of lives. From the deserts of Namibia to the razor-backed Himalayas, there are wonderful creatures that have roamed Earth much longer than we, creatures that not only are worthy of our respect but could teach us about ourselves.

2   Some of those wilds I know personally, at the level of sand, orchid, wingless fly, human being. So each photograph is an album, a palimpsest, a pageant. There is Torishima, the little island south of Tokyo, which is the final stronghold of short-tailed albatrosses. There is French Frigate Shoals, the last refuge of the Hawaiian monk seal. There is Antarctica, home to vast herds of animals. While I look at a photograph of the Hawaiian Islands—puddles of ink on a bright copper sea—I remember the sound and rumble of humpback-whale song cresting over me as I swam. Humpback whales have had a civilization without cities, a kind of roaming culture, for many ages. They live in the ocean as in a wide blue cave. They pass on an oral tradition, teach one another their songs, abandon old versions, use rhyme. Our recordings of them go back to 1951, but after more than forty years, the whales haven't returned to their original songs of the fifties. Just imagine the arias, ballads, and cantatas of ancient days that have filled the oceans with song, then died out, never to be heard again. Today we can visit the campfires of a few remaining tribes of Stone Age people and hear the stories they tell, stories marvelous, imaginative, and rich with wonder. But we will never know all the lost stories of the cave people. The same may be true of humpback whales. As I page through the book, I feast on habitats far-flung and dizzying. Life haunts every one of them, no matter how distant, dry, hot, salty, or sunless.

The photograph of Africa reminds me of the giant animals caged forever in the past. The large animals we associate with Africa—elephants, giraffes, hippos, ostriches, and others—are dwindling remnants of the massive creatures that once flourished…. When I look at the photographs of Borneo, Brazil, and New Guinea, I remember how the dynamic well of the rain forests has generated new life-forms. Our genetic safety net is woven from their biodiversity.

Write an essay in which you explain how Diane Ackerman builds an argument to persuade her audience. In your essay, analyze how Ackerman uses one or more of the features in the directions that precede the passage (or features of your own choice) to strengthen the logic and persuasiveness of her argument. Be sure that your analysis focuses on the most relevant features of the passage.

Your essay should not explain whether you agree with Ackerman's claims, but rather explain how Ackerman builds an argument to persuade her audience.

S: Ackerman appears to be a naturalist, though we cannot be sure that she is a scientist.

O: mankind's current place within environmental history

A: general audience

P: to inspire serious concern regarding mankind's prospects for extinction

S: We are not special in the grand scheme of history; we, too, are vulnerable.

Leafing idly through *The Home Planet*, I stop at a picture of Earth floating against the black velvet of space. Africa and Europe are visible under swirling white clouds, but the predominant color is blue.	***Imagery***: *While not a developed story, Ackerman's experience leafing through a book of photographs introduces her inspiration for the essay and personalizes her points. The description she gives of the planet Earth has poetic flourishes, indicating its beauty in the eyes of the author. Throughout this piece of writing, Ackerman's depictions of the Earth's beauty shows her reader what is at stake if humans are inattentive.*
This was the one picture from the *Apollo* missions that told the whole story—how small the planet is in the vast sprawl of space, how fragile its environments are. Seen from space, Earth has no national borders, no military zones, no visible fences. Quite the opposite. You can see how storm systems swirling above a continent may well affect the grain yield half a world away. The entire atmosphere of the planet—all the air we breathe, all the sky we fly through, even the ozone layer—is visible as the thinnest rind.	***Imagery and Depth of Observation***: *Ackerman makes several observations here about how small the Earth is relative to space, and how fragile it is; she also notes that Earth from this distance has no political markings.*
The picture eloquently reminds us that Earth is a single organism.	***Claim/Comparison***: *Ackerman's prior statements describing the lack of visible divisions on the face of the Earth lead up to this claim about the Earth's unity and likening it to a single organism.*
For me, the book contains visual mnemonics of how I feel about nature. At some point, one asks, "Toward what end is my life lived?" A great freedom comes from being able to answer that question. A sleeper can be decoyed out of bed by the sheer beauty of dawn on the open seas.	***Appeal to Emotion***: *Ackerman shares her feelings as she looks at the photos, as well as a profound question that people ask themselves.*
Part of my job, as I see it, is to allow that to happen. Sleepers like me need at some point to rise and take their turn on morning watch, for the sake of the planet, but also for their own sake, for the enrichment of lives.	***Comparison***: *Ackerman here implies that people, including herself, need to take responsibility for the planet's well-being not only for it but for themselves. She refers to herself and others as "sleepers," asserting that we need to "wake up."*
From the deserts of Namibia to the razor-backed Himalayas, there are wonderful creatures that have roamed Earth much longer than we, creatures that not only are worthy of our respect but could teach us about ourselves.	***Evidence and claim***: *Ackerman gives examples of the various landscapes and their inhabitants to which we should be attentive; she reiterates her claim that people need to respect nature and in turn learn about themselves.*

SOAPS AND APPEALS DRILL 3

Again read the prompt and the excerpt, looking for SOAPS and rhetorical devices.

> **Excerpted from *Who grows your food? (And why it matters),* an article by Bob Schildgen that originally appeared in the November/December 2004 issue of *Sierra* magazine. www.sierramagazine.org.**

1   We [environmentalists] criticize farmers for the use of polluting pesticides and fertilizers; for robbing wildlife of water by pulling it from rivers and aquifers for irrigation; for damaging streams and causing erosion through bad grazing practices; and for erasing wildlife habitat. We condemn agriculture for poisoning wells in the Midwest and California's Central Valley, and blame it for the dead zone in the Gulf of Mexico, where the Mississippi dumps toxic runoff from a third of the U.S. landmass.

2   Such criticism usually doesn't sit too well with the farmers themselves. After all, they are feeding us, and doing it as efficiently as they know how. It often sounds as if we're yelling at them across a cultural gap.

3   Fortunately, some farmers are now bridging this gap, with help from those environmentalists who support sustainable agriculture. Farmers like the Dubas family from eastern Nebraska...are trying environmentally friendly methods and selling their products locally. They're running a diversified operation, rotating crops, keeping plenty of land in pasture, and raising their livestock without routinely dosing them with antibiotics.

4   The history of the Dubas family is one that has played out across rural America. Ron Dubas's father made a living on 200 to 300 acres. Today, the family runs 2,000 acres and struggles to keep afloat. Four hundred miles northeast, on the northern edge of the corn belt in Wisconsin's unglaciated prairie, my grandparents got by on 80 acres. Now farms up there are often five times that size. The number of real producing farms nationwide has shrunk from 3.3 million in 1950 to 750,000 today.

5   What explains this decline? Price, mainly. You can't afford to stay in business if your costs exceed what you're paid for your product. In 1998, for example, hog prices plummeted—from 45 cents a pound to less than 10 cents a pound, only one-fourth the cost of production. Customers in the supermarket had no way of noticing: The price of a pork chop fell by only pennies.

6   What's this got to do with the environment? Well, farmers can cope by producing more, in the hope that volume will make up for low prices. Or they can switch to other commodities, but they'll likely raise them in high volume to cover previous losses. Either way, they're forced to resort to more intensive cultivation and more irrigation, fertilizers, and pesticides. They have long been encouraged to do this by the agricultural establishment. Universities supplied the research and technical assistance to ramp up production, lending agencies the capital, and government the subsidies. For years the mantra was "Get big or get out," and Richard Nixon's agriculture secretary exhorted, "Plant fencerow to fencerow."

7   But this "efficiency" has a high cost. As production soared, prices generally dropped, encouraging more production. The math is simple. Consider corn. In 1955, a farmer got $1.43 a bushel. Adjusted for inflation, that bushel should be worth over $9 today, but the price hovers around $2 or $3. Although the yield has almost tripled since the 1950s, this increase hasn't kept pace with rising expenses, like taxes, mortgages, fertilizers, and pesticides. Moreover, half of that increased yield, according to research at Purdue University, has come from increased use of nitrogen fertilizers, a major source of pollution.

8   The biggest beneficiaries of the farmers' cornucopia are the agribusiness corporations that absorb the glut of cheap raw material and turn it into our dazzlingly diverse (and dangerously unhealthy) supply of processed foods. Take soft drinks made with cheap corn sweeteners. Sixty years ago, each American consumed an average of 60 12-ounce servings of soda a year. Today, we're guzzling almost ten times that much. Yesterday's occasional treat has exploded into a regular diet of 64-ounce Double Gulps.

9   As food-processing profits have grown, the farmer's average share of food income has shrunk. In 1950, farmers got 50 cents out of every retail food dollar; now they receive less than 20 cents. The rest goes to processing, distribution, and marketing. While thousands of farmers take outside jobs to survive, advertisers spend $28 billion a year just to promote food products. To illustrate the triumph of marketing over honest toil: The corn in a one-pound, $4 box of cornflakes costs about four cents. The retailer is paid eight cents to process a coupon for this box. Yes, the farmer gets half as much as the coupon shufflers.

S: an environmentalist

O: the state of agriculture in the modern Western world

A: other environmentalists

P: to explain how farmers have been disadvantaged by modern industrial farming practices and to inspire understanding; also, to show hope for the future (Dubas family)

S: Environmentalists and farmers need a greater understanding of each other's priorities and challenges. Modern industrial agriculture does not benefit farmers economically and may slow the development of more sustainable methods.

We [environmentalists] criticize farmers for the use of polluting pesticides and fertilizers; for robbing wildlife of water by pulling it from rivers and aquifers for irrigation; for damaging streams and causing erosion through bad grazing practices; and for erasing wildlife habitat. We condemn agriculture for poisoning wells in the Midwest and California's Central Valley, and blame it for the dead zone in the Gulf of Mexico, where the Mississippi dumps toxic runoff from a third of the U.S. landmass.

Audience: Schildgen establishes right away that his audience already agrees with a few of the claims in paragraph 1. He is speaking to environmentalists. He is establishing common ground with the audience, but he will later raise issues they may not have considered.

Such criticism usually doesn't sit too well with the farmers themselves. After all, they are feeding us, and doing it as efficiently as they know how.

Appeal to Emotion

yelling at them across a cultural gap
Farmers like the Dubas family from eastern Nebraska...are trying environmentally friendly methods and selling their products locally. They're running a diversified operation, rotating crops, keeping plenty of land in pasture, and raising their livestock without routinely dosing them with antibiotics.

Metaphor

Anecdote: The example of the Dubas family helps to persuade the reader that environmentally friendly changes to agriculture are possible.

Ron Dubas's father made a living on 200 to 300 acres. Today, the family runs 2,000 acres and struggles to keep afloat. Four hundred miles northeast, on the northern edge of the corn belt in Wisconsin's unglaciated prairie, my grandparents got by on 80 acres. Now farms up there are often five times that size. The number of real producing farms nationwide has shrunk from 3.3 million in 1950 to 750,000 today.

Appeal to Logic: Through specific examples and statistical data, the author persuades us that farming has changed.

In 1998, for example, hog prices plummeted-from 45 cents a pound to less than 10 cents a pound, only one-fourth the cost of production.

Appeal to Logic

The math is simple. Consider corn. In 1955, a farmer got $1.43 a bushel. Adjusted for inflation, that bushel should be worth over $9 today, but the price hovers around $2 or $3. Although the yield has almost tripled since the 1950s, this increase hasn't kept pace with rising expenses, like taxes, mortgages, fertilizers, and pesticides.

Appeal to Logic: statistics and comparing time periods to show a general trend

Double Gulps

Allusion: to point out the absurdity of the modern food industry?

As food-processing profits have grown, the farmer's average share of food income has shrunk. In 1950, farmers got 50 cents out of every retail food dollar; now they receive less than 20 cents. The rest goes to processing, distribution, and marketing. While thousands of farmers take outside jobs to survive, advertisers spend $28 billion a year just to promote food products. To illustrate the triumph of marketing over honest toil: The corn in a one-pound, $4 box of cornflakes costs about four cents. The retailer is paid eight cents to process a coupon for this box. Yes, the farmer gets half as much as the coupon shufflers.

Appeal to Logic: statistics and more time comparisons to invoke sympathy for the plight of farmers

TASK 3: WRITING

The final task of the Essay test is to actually write the essay. According to the College Board, this requires you to

- make use of a central claim.
- use effective organization and progression of ideas.
- use varied sentence structures.
- employ precise word choice.
- maintain consistent, appropriate style and tone.
- show command of the conventions of standard written English.

This is also where you show your grader that you have read, understood, and analyzed the text.

Essay Template

Introduction

Your introduction needs to do three things:

1. Describe the text. This is where you'll bring in the SOAPS points. This can be done in one sentence.
2. Paraphrase the argument. This is where you'll show your grader that you understand the text by concisely summing up the main points and the overall message of the text. The Reading score comes from your demonstration of comprehension of the text.
3. Introduce the examples you will be discussing in the body paragraphs. You will establish a framework in your introduction that you should then follow for the rest of the essay.

Body Paragraphs

The body paragraphs will focus on different appeals or style elements the author uses to effectively communicate the argument. Each body paragraph will need to do the following:

1. Name and explain the rhetorical device or appeal.
   a. Where is it in the text?
   b. Use short, relevant quotes to show you understand the text and the rhetorical device, but do not rely on long excerpts from the passage. In order to get a high score, you need to use your words to explain what's going on.
2. Identify the effects of the author's rhetorical choices.
   a. Explain the connection between the rhetorical device/appeal and the text, and your argument in general. Do not simply quote chunks of text and then briefly paraphrase. Your goal is to answer the question, "How does this contribute to the author's argument?"

b. For example:
   i. Do not simply say, "This is an example of imagery."
   ii. Explain why the imagery is effective. Perhaps the author's descriptions of the beautiful sunset effectively draw in the reader, creating an emotional connection between the author and her audience. This connection may make the audience more sympathetic to the author's subsequent points because there is an emotional connection now.
c. Explaining how the device or appeal works is how you show your grader your ability to analyze the text.

Conclusion
1. Restate the goal of the text and briefly paraphrase the elements you discussed in your essay.
2. Be concise and accurate.

ESSAY CHECKLIST
Check your essay for

1. An introductory paragraph
   Does your introductory paragraph contain a strong topic sentence, one that lets the reader know what the paper will discuss? Does your introductory paragraph mention what examples your paper will include?

2. Body paragraphs
   Does each body paragraph contain a nice clear transition sentence? Does each body paragraph develop one or multiple similar examples? Did you include short quotes?

3. A conclusion
   Your essay has a conclusion, right? Did you restate your main ideas? Did you summarize how your quotes are relevant?

WRITING TIPS!
- Maintain a formal style and objective tone. Avoid "I" and "you." No slang.
- Use varied sentence structure.
- Write neatly.
- Use clear transitions.
- Use short, relevant quotes from the text.
- Don't worry about official terms for things. "Appeal to the emotions" is fine instead of specifically referencing "pathos," and "comparison of two things" is okay instead of referring to a metaphor. If you *do* know the official terms, though, feel free to use them!

PACING

You have 50 minutes for the essay. Spend the first 5 to 10 minutes reading the prompt and brainstorming examples.

Use the next 40–45 minutes to write your essay. Aim for a five- or six-paragraph essay, with an introduction, three to four body paragraphs, and a conclusion. Stay focused on the topic, and keep things simple.

Take the last five minutes to proofread your essay. Watch out for grammar mistakes—one or two may be okay, but too many of them will hurt your Writing score. If you're unsure how to spell a word, choose a different one.

The visual appearance of your essay is important as well. While you should avoid double-spacing or otherwise puffing up your essay, it helps to indent your paragraphs, neatly erase any mistakes, and write as legibly as you can manage. If you make the reader's job easier, you're more likely to get a better score.

Appendix

PREPOSITION LIST

Prepositions are everywhere in our language, but you don't need to know every preposition in the world to do well on the SAT. In fact, there are really only a handful of prepositions that are regularly tested, but keep your eyes peeled for these, as seeing one could mean a prepositional phrase or an idiom.

- about
- above
- after
- against
- among
- around
- as
- at
- before
- behind
- below
- beneath
- beside(s)
- between
- beyond
- but
- by
- despite
- down
- during
- except
- for
- from
- in
- inside
- into
- like
- of
- off
- on
- onto
- outside
- over
- per
- regarding
- since
- than
- through
- to
- toward
- towards
- under
- underneath
- unlike
- until
- up
- upon
- versus
- with
- within
- without

IDIOM LIST

Here's a list of the idioms tested most frequently on the SAT. Learn them!

About

Worry...about

If you **worry** too much **about** the SAT, you'll develop an ulcer.

As

Define...as

Some people **define** insanity **as** repeating the same action but expecting a different outcome.

Regard...as

Art historians **regard** the *Mona Lisa* **as** one of the greatest works of art.

Not so...as

He is **not so** much smart **as** cunning.

So...as to be

She is **so** beautiful **as to be** exquisite.

Think of...as

Think of it more **as** a promise than a threat.

See...as

Many people **see** euthanasia **as** an escape from pain.

The same...as

Mom and Dad gave **the same** punishment to me **as** to you.

As...as

Memorizing idioms is not **as** fun **as** playing bingo.

At

Target...at

The commercials were obviously **targeted at** teenage boys.

For

Responsible for

You are **responsible for** the child.

From

Prohibit...from

He was **prohibited from** entering the public library after he accidentally set the dictionary on fire with a magnifying glass.

Different...from

There are some who argue that Chicago's deep-dish pizza is not so **different from** New York City's pan pizza.

Over

Dispute over

The men had a **dispute over** money.

That

So...that

He was **so** late **that** he missed the main course.

Hypothesis...that

The **hypothesis that** aspartame causes brain tumors has not been proven yet.

To be

Believe...to be

His friends do not **believe** the ring he bought at the auction **to be** Lady Gaga's; they all think he was tricked.

Estimate to be

The time he has spent impersonating Elvis is **estimated to be** longer than the time Elvis himself spent performing.

To

Forbid...to

I **forbid** you **to** call me before noon.

Ability to

If you take the test enough times, you might develop the **ability to** choose the credited responses without reading the questions.

Attribute to

Many amusing quips are **attributed to** Anna Kendrick.

Require to

Before you enter the house you are **required to** take off your hat.

Responsibility to

Reporters have a **responsibility to** accurately relay the news.

Permit...to

I don't **permit** my children **to** play with knives in the living room.

Superior to

My pasta sauce is far **superior to** my mother-in-law's.

Try to

Try to stay awake during the essay section of the test.

With

Credit...with

Many people **credit** Christopher Columbus **with** the discovery of America, but Native Americans were here first.

Associate with

Most politicians prefer not to be **associated with** the Mafia.

Contrast...with

My father likes to **contrast** my grades **with** my brother's.

No preposition

Consider...(nothing)

Art historians **consider** the *Mona Lisa* one of the greatest works of art.

More than one preposition

Distinguish...from

I can't **distinguish** day **from** night.

Distinguish between...and

I can **distinguish** between black **and** white.

Native (noun) of

Russell Crowe is a **native of** Australia.

Native (adjective) to

The kangaroo is **native to** Australia.

Comparisons and Links

Not only...but also

She is **not only** beautiful, **but also** smart.

Not...but

The review was **not** mean-spirited **but** merely flippant.

Either...or

I must have **either** chocolate ice cream **or** carrot cake to complete a grand meal.

Neither...nor

Because Jenny was grounded, she could **neither** leave the house **nor** use the telephone.

Both...and

When given the choice, I choose **both** ice cream **and** cake.

More...than; Less...than

The chimpanzee is much **more** intelligent **than** the orangutan.

As vs. like

As is used to compare actions.

Like is used to compare nouns.

He did not vote for the Libertarian Party, **as** I did.

Her coat is just **like** mine.

Like vs. such as

Like means *similar to*.

Such as means *for example*.

The mule, **like** the donkey, is a close relative of the horse.

Many of my favorite ice cream flavors, **such as** chocolate chip and strawberry, are also available as frozen yogurt.

The more...the –er

The more you ignore me, the **louder** I get.

From...to

Scores on the SAT range **from** 400 **to** 1600.

Just as...so too

Just as I crossed over to the dark side, **so too** will you, my son.

Miscellaneous

Each vs. all or both

Use *each* when you want to emphasize the separateness of the items.

Use *both* (for two things) or *all* (for more than two things) when you want to emphasize the togetherness of the items.

> **Each** of the doctors had his own specialty.

> **Both** of the women went to Bryn Mawr for their undergraduate degrees.

> **All** of the letters received before January 15 went into the drawing for the $10 million prize.

Whether vs. if

Use *whether* when there are *two possibilities*.

Use *if* in *conditional statements*.

> Eduardo wasn't sure **whether** he could make it to the party.

> **If** Eduardo comes to the party, he will bring a bag of chips.

Yes, These are Real Words

Sometimes the SAT likes to use big words to frighten you. If you see these in an Improving Sentences or Improving Paragraphs question, see if the SAT has given you an option to use a simpler, more direct word.

Furthermore	Nonetheless
Heretofore	Notwithstanding
Hereinafter	Ought
Inasmuch	Ongoing
Insofar	Therefore
Likewise	Thereby
Moreover	Whereas
Nevertheless	Whereby

Paying for
College 101

If you're reading this book, you've already made an investment in your education. You may have shelled out some cold, hard cash for this book, and you've definitely invested time in reading it. It's probably even safe to say that this is one of the smaller investments you've made in your future so far. You put in the hours and hard work needed to keep up your GPA. You've paid test fees and applications fees, perhaps even travel expenses. You have probably committed time and effort to a host of extracurricular activities to make sure colleges know that you're a well-rounded student.

But after you get in, there's one more issue to think about: how do you pay for college?

Let's be honest: college is not cheap. The average cost for tuition and fees for a private four-year college is over $35,000 a year. The average cost for tuition and fees at a four-year public school is about $9,000 a year. And the cost is rising. Every year the sticker price of college education bumps up about 6 percent.

More Great Titles from The Princeton Review
Paying for College Without Going Broke
The Best 384 Colleges

Like many of us, your family may not have 35 grand sitting around in a shoebox. With such a hefty price tag, you might be wondering "Is a college education really worth it?" The short answer: Yes! No question about it. According to the U.S. Bureau of Labor Statistics, the median weekly earnings of full-time workers with bachelor's degrees were $1,173 in 2017, compared with $712 for those workers who finished only high school. That adds up to a difference of almost $23,000 a year!

Still, the cost of college is no joke. It's said that a college education ultimately pays for itself; however, some pay better than others. It's best to be prudent when determining the amount of debt that is reasonable for you to take on.

Here's the good news. Even in the wake of the current financial crisis, financial aid is available to almost any student who wants it. There is an estimated $177 billion—that's right, billion!—in financial aid offered to students annually. This comes in the form of federal grants, scholarships, state financed aid, loans, and other programs.

We know that financial aid can seem like an overwhelmingly complex issue, but the introductory information in this chapter should help you grasp what's available and get you started in your search.

How Much Does College Really Cost?

When most people think about the price of a college education, they think of one thing and one thing alone: tuition. It's time to get that notion out of your head. While tuition is a significant portion of the cost of a college education, you need to think of all the other things that factor into the final price tag.

Let's break it down.

- Tuition and fees
- Room and board
- Books and supplies
- Personal expenses
- Travel expenses

Collectively, these things contribute to your total Cost of Attendance (COA) for one year at a college or university.

Understanding the distinction between tuition and COA is crucial because it will help you understand this simple equation:

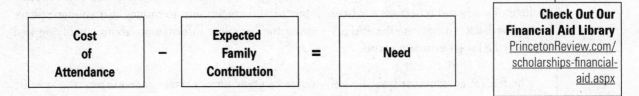

| Cost of Attendance | − | Expected Family Contribution | = | Need |

Check Out Our Financial Aid Library
PrincetonReview.com/scholarships-financial-aid.aspx

When you begin the financial aid process, you will see this equation again and again. We've already talked about the COA, so let's talk about the Estimated Family Contribution, or EFC. The EFC simply means, "How much you and your family can afford to pay for college." Sounds obvious right?

Here's the catch: what you think you can afford to pay for college, what the government thinks you can afford to pay for college, and what a college or university thinks you can afford to pay for college are, unfortunately, three different things. Keep that in mind as we discuss financing options later on.

The final term in the equation is self-explanatory. Anything that's left after what you and your family have contributed still needs to be covered. That's where financial aid packages come in.

WHAT'S IN A FINANCIAL AID PACKAGE?

A typical financial aid package contains money—from the school, federal government, or state—in various forms: grants, scholarships, work-study programs, and loans.

Let's look at the non-loan options first. Non-loan options include grants, scholarships, and work-study programs. The crucial thing about them is that they involve monetary assistance that you won't be asked to pay back. They are as close as you'll get to "free money."

Grants

Grants are basically gifts. They are funds given to you by the federal government, state agencies, or individual colleges. They are usually need-based, and you are not required to pay them back.

One of the most important grants is the Pell Grant. Pell Grants are provided by the federal government but administered through individual schools. Amounts can change yearly. The maximum Federal Pell Grant award is $6,095 for the 2018–19 award year.

You apply for a Pell Grant by filling out the Free Application for Federal Student Aid (FAFSA). Remember that acronym because you'll be seeing it again. Completing the FAFSA is the first step in applying for any federal aid. The FAFSA can be found online at www.fafsa.ed.gov.

There are several other major federal grant programs that hand out grants ranging from $100 to thousands of dollars annually. Some of these grants are given to students entering a specific field of study and others are need-based, but all of them amount to money that you never have to pay back. Check out the FAFSA website for complete information about qualifying and applying for government grants.

The federal government isn't the only source of grant money. State governments and specific schools also offer grants. Use the Internet, your guidance counselor, and your library to see what non-federal grants you might be eligible for.

Scholarships

Like grants, you never have to pay a scholarship back. But the requirements and terms of a scholarship might vary wildly. Most scholarships are merit- or need-based, but they can be based on almost anything. There are scholarships based on academic performance, athletic achievements, musical or artistic talent, religious affiliation, ethnicity, and so on.

When hunting for scholarships, one great place to start is the U.S. Department of Labor's "Scholarship Search," available at www.careerinfonet.org/scholarshipsearch. It includes over 5,000 scholarships, fellowships, loans, and other opportunities. It's a free service and a great resource.

Check Out the Scholarship Search Page
https://www.princeton-review.com/college-advice/finding-college-scholarships

The Bottom Line? Not So Fast!
It is possible to appeal the amount of the financial aid package a school awards you. To learn more about how to do that, check out "Appealing Your Award Package" at https://www.princetonreview.com/college-advice/appealing-financial-aid-award

There is one important caveat about taking scholarship money. Some, but not all, schools think of scholarship money as income and will reduce the amount of aid they offer you accordingly. Know your school's policy on scholarship awards.

Federal Work-Study (FWS)

One of the ways Uncle Sam disperses aid money is by subsidizing part-time jobs, usually on campus, for students who need financial aid. Because your school will administer the money, they get to decide what your work-study job will be. Work-study participants are paid by the hour, and federal law requires that they cannot be paid less than the federal minimum wage.

One of the benefits of a work-study program is that you get a paycheck just like you would at a normal job. The money is intended to go toward school expenses, but there are no controls over exactly how you spend it.

Colleges and universities determine how to administer work-study programs on their own campuses.

LOANS

Most likely, your entire COA won't be covered by scholarships, grants, and work-study income. The next step in gathering the necessary funds is securing a loan. Broadly speaking, there are two routes to go: federal loans and private loans. Once upon a time, which route to choose might be open for debate. But these days the choice is clear: *always* try to secure federal loans first. Almost without exception, federal loans provide unbeatable low fixed-interest rates; they come with generous repayment terms; and, although they have lending limits, these limits are quite generous and will take you a long way toward your goal. We'll talk about the benefits of private loans later, but they really can't measure up to what the government can provide and should be considered a last resort.

Stafford Loans

The Stafford loan is the primary form of federal student loan. Loans can be subsidized or unsubsidized. Students with demonstrated financial need may qualify for subsidized loans. This means that the government pays interest accumulated during the time the student is in school. Students with unsubsidized Stafford loans are responsible for the interest accumulated while in school. You can qualify for a subsidized Stafford loan, an unsubsidized Stafford loan, or a mixture of the two.

Stafford loans are available to all full-time students and most part-time students. Though the terms of the loan are based on demonstrated financial need, lack of need is not considered grounds for rejection. No payment is expected while the student is attending school. The interest rate on your Stafford loan will depend on when your first disbursement is.

As with grants, you must start by completing the Free Application for Federal Student Aid (FAFSA) to apply for a Stafford loan.

PLUS Loans

Another important federal loan is the PLUS loan, which is designed to help parents and guardians put dependent students through college. Unlike the Stafford loan, the PLUS has no fixed limits or fixed interest rates. The annual limit on a PLUS loan is equal to your COA minus any other financial aid you are already receiving. It may be used on top of a Stafford loan. The interest rates on PLUS loans are variable though often comparable to, or even lower than, the interest rates on Stafford loans. Your PLUS Loan enters repayment once your loan is fully disbursed (paid out).

To become eligible for a PLUS loan, you need only complete a Free Application for Federal Student Aid (FAFSA). There are no other special requirements or forms to fill out.

Perkins Loans

A third and final federal loan you should be aware of is the Perkins loan. Intended to help students in extreme need, the Perkins loan is a government-subsidized loan that is administered only through college and university financial aid offices. Under the terms of a Perkins loan, you may borrow up to $5,500 a year of undergraduate study, up to $27,500. The Perkins loan has a fixed interest rate of just 5 percent. Payments against the loan don't start until nine months after you graduate. Apply for Perkins loans through your school's financial aid office.

Private Lenders

We said it before, and we'll say it again: DO NOT get a private loan until you've exhausted all other options.

That said, there are *some* benefits to securing a private loan. First off, many students find that non-loan and federal loan options don't end up covering the entire bill. If that's the case, then private lenders might just save the day. Second, loans from private sources generally offer you greater flexibility with how you use the funds. Third, private loans can be taken out at anytime during your academic career. Unlike most non-loan and government-backed financial options, you can turn to private lenders whenever you need them.

All private lenders are not the same! As the old song says, "You better shop around." Every lender is going to offer you a different package of terms. What you need to do is find the package that best fits your needs and plans. Aside from low interest rates, which are crucially important, there other terms and conditions you will want to look for.

Low origination fees

Origination fees are fees that lenders charge you for taking out a loan. Usually the fee is simply deducted automatically from your loan checks. Obviously, the lower the origination fee, the better.

Minimal guaranty fees

A guaranty fee is an amount you pay to a third party who agrees to insure your loan. That way, if the borrower—that is you—can't pay the loan back, the guarantor steps in and pays the difference. Again, if you can minimize or eliminate this fee, all the better.

Interest rate reductions

Some lenders will reduce your interest rates if you're reliable with your payments. Some will even agree to knock a little off the interest rate if you agree to pay your loans through a direct deposit system. When shopping for the best loan, pay careful attention to factors that might help you curb your interest rates.

Flexible payment plans

One of the great things about most federal loans is the fact that you don't have to start paying them off until you leave school. In order to compete, many private lenders have been forced to adopt similarly flexible payment plans. Before saying yes to a private loan, make sure that it comes with a payment timetable you can live with.

IT'S YOUR CALL

No matter what the state of the economy, it is always a good idea to thoroughly research the assortment of low-interest federal assistance programs available to you. Weigh your financing options (loans, grants, scholarships, work study, etc.) against the overall cost of your college education. Remember that this is a personal choice with potentially long-term ramifications, and that what your peers are doing may not be right for you. Talk it over with your parent(s) or guardian(s). With thoughtful planning (and a lot of form-filling!), it's possible to pay your way though school without breaking the bank.

NOTES

NOTES

NOTES

NOTES